CRITICAL ACCLAIM
FOR GUTSY WOMEN

"The book is essential reading for women travelers of any age."
—*Chicago Tribune*

"The perfect bon voyage gift for your favorite woman traveler."
—*Living Fit Magazine*

"A nuts-and-bolts approach to women's travel…seasoned advice geared both to novices and veterans."
—*USA Today*

"Packed with instructive and inspiring travel vignettes and tips…it is not just for adventure seekers or solo travelers."
—*Boston Globe*

"How do you cope with an impulse to take wing? How do you handle desires to find adventures in exotic cultures…? If you're Marybeth Bond, you promptly leap aboard such urges, ride them where they happen to take you, then seek to lead others by word and example."
—*San Francisco Chronicle*

"If you've got the bug to get out but are leery of the less-beaten path, check out *Gutsy Women*. Bond has packed this paperback with handy advice."
—*Women's Sports & Fitness*

"Fresh and insightful, even for the most-seasoned traveler."
—*Washington Post*

"*Gutsy Women* is a wonderful gift for a woman traveling…and features engaging stories and personal advice by women travelers…"
—*Chicago Herald*

Gutsy Women

more travel tips and wisdom for the road

Gutsy Women

more travel tips and wisdom for the road

Third Edition

MARYBETH BOND

Travelers' Tales
Palo Alto

Travelers' Tales and Solas House are trademarks of Solas House, Inc., 853 Alma
Street, Palo Alto, California 94301. www.travelerstales.com

Cover design: Stefan Gutermuth
Cover illustration: Melissa Sweet
Interior design: Susan Bailey
Page layout: Cynthia Lamb using the fonts Berkeley Book, Wade Sans Light,
and Gill Sans.

Library of Congress Cataloging-in-Publication Data

Bond, Marybeth.
    Gutsy women: more travel tips and wisdom for the road / Marybeth Bond.
    —3rd ed.
        p. cm.
    Includes bibliographic references and index.
    ISBN 1-932361-51-0 (pbk.)
    1. Travel. 2. Women travelers. I. Title.

G151.B66 2007
910.2'02—dc22

                                    2007016420

Third Edition
Printed in the United States
10 9 8 7 6 5 4 3 2 1

*For my husband, Gary, and
my children, Julieclaire and Annalyse,
for encouraging me to fulfill my passion to travel—with and
without them.*

TABLE OF CONTENTS

INTRODUCTION

WHAT'S A GUTSY WOMAN? To me, gutsy means courageous and women today are courageous in a twenty-first century way. We buy our own cars, homes, diamonds, and we are open to adventure—whether it's climbing Mt. Everest, biking across the USA, or running for a "cause." Gutsy women are bold, strong and savvy, not foolish and naïve. The tips and wisdom that fill the pages of this edition of *Gutsy Women* will empower, energize, and inspire you. Even if you're not sure if you are a Gutsy Woman, this book will allow you to discover her within you.

In terms of travel, our habits have changed too. After all, women make 80 percent of the travel decisions, and we're on the go. We are getting off the beaten track and trekking the globe, on our own and with other women.

If your partner isn't interested in traveling, or not to the places you may want to visit, then I encourage you to find friends who are. If a friend is too busy or your schedules don't synch, book yourself on an all-women's tour and you'll probably meet some travel companions for your next adventure. Your first trip without the company of a close friend or spouse doesn't have to be to the other side of the world. It can be a journey close to home— somewhere you've always wanted to go—somewhere just to get your feet wet. Even if you are already a seasoned traveler, I'm sure you will learn something new and useful in this expanded edition of *Gutsy Women*.

Over the past thirty years I have hiked, cycled, climbed, dived, and kayaked my way through more than seventy countries, from the depths of the Flores Sea to the summit of Mount Kilimanjaro. I traveled alone around the world for two years at the age of twenty-nine, wandered the globe with my husband (who I met in Kathmandu when I was thirty), and more recently I have explored this bountiful and beautiful earth with my daughters and girl-friends.

In the process of creating ten travel books, including nine for Travelers' Tales and one for National Geographic, I have discovered what women want in their travel experiences: safety, freedom, adventure, opportunities for learning and giving back, and time to nurture ourselves. I have interviewed hundreds of gutsy women who have shared their stories, their wisdom, and their strength with me and through this book with you, too.

The information you will find within this new edition speaks to a broad group of women travelers. I've updated the tips and added many more—making sure to include the most useful information for women, to help you prepare for your trip online and offline, and insure you have a safe and memorable journey.

The wisdom in this book is for women of all ages. Whether you are a young, first-time voyager at age sixteen or a seasoned world traveler, you will discover that women help and inspire each other before the journey and while on the road. Seek out the community of women—a worldwide network exists—and know that these new connections will enhance your travels.

The power of travel for women is that we come away from our trips with an enhanced positive sense of self.

So be a gutsy women and go forth to change yourself and the world.

I
The First Step

The impulse to travel is one of the hopeful symptoms of life.
—*Agnes Repplier*

BEFORE WE DO ANYTHING IN LIFE, even the most impulsive of us do some preparation. We educate ourselves to prepare for careers, plan strategies for important meetings, make menus for simple or extravagant meals. Preparation helps us reduce fears by giving us knowledge and builds confidence by increasing our comfort with the unknown.

Preparing yourself mentally and emotionally for traveling overseas is just as important as getting your visas and shots. Give yourself time to work through fears you may have about safety, traveling alone or in a group of unknown companions, or fitting into a different culture. To convert your apprehension into excitement, begin your mental preparation weeks or even months prior to departure. Get in touch with women who have gone before you. They will be your role models. Connect with them by phone, e-mail, or by reading their stories in travel books.

It is reassuring before you take your trip to have an itinerary, guidebooks, research from the Internet, and detailed notes from friends who have been there before. I've found that the most valuable sources of up-to-date information are other travelers you'll meet along the way, locals you will encounter on trains or at bus stops, or the staff at tourist offices, hotels, and bed-and-breakfasts. Fight the urge to

---

What do you love? If your passion is cooking, consider a New Orleans, Paris, or Provence Culinary experience. If you love gardening, a green thumb is not required to enjoy Holland in Bloom or the Chelsea Flower Show. Compare all your travel options and listen to your heart.

♦

Marybeth Bond

organize everything before you go. Spontaneity and flexibility are the creative forces behind meaningful journeys. Try to avoid overscheduling and overplanning.

When I left on my around-the-world journey, I had a detailed itinerary. I abandoned it on day three in Bangkok. If I had followed my original plans, I never would have met Danielle, a Swiss nurse with whom I traveled for a month, stayed with a Muslim family on a houseboat in Kashmir, or hiked for a week with another new travel friend among the ethnic tribes of northern Thailand. It is tempting to follow a structured itinerary on long or short trips. Recently, on a weeklong trip to Paris, I lost all the notes a friend gave me with restaurant and shopping recommendations. Instead of reliving her trip, I discovered my own, more relaxed version of the City of Lights. I dined *en plein air* at a sidewalk restaurant on the seventeenth-century Place des Vosges and visited three museums in one day, instead of searching for my friend's favorite shops.

We discover the world as we physically move around the planet; we discover ourselves on the inner journey that accompanies our travels. The rewards are many: We try on new identities as more independent, self-sufficient women; we explore new behaviors; and we develop a greater awareness of our potential.

The trick is not to rid your stomach of butterflies, but to make them fly in formation.

Pacific Crest Outward Bound School, Book of Readings

Remind yourself that the minimal risk of traveling is far outweighed by the rewards.

TIPS

➤ Buy your airline tickets on Tuesday or Wednesday. Although it is not always the case, here's the typical scenario: An airline announces a fare sale on Monday, and on Tuesday other airlines match the price or undercut it. On Wednesday, the fare war is in high gear. By Thursday most of the cheap fares are gone.

Saturday is the worst day to buy a ticket. Airlines usually raise their prices late on Friday night to see if other airlines will, too. If no one follows suit, then fares may go back down by Monday.

➤ Do your research. Begin at your public library or online. Search by subject matter or country name for a listing of all magazine and newspaper articles, historical and political studies, novels, documentaries, and movies about the destination you are visiting. Check out books or videos well in advance of your journey.

As a woman, my fear of being cooped up in my home without new challenges, new conversations, new vistas, far outweighs any fears I might have of traveling solo in a strange land.

◆

Evelyn Hannon,
Toronto, Canada

➤ Put travel anthologies on your reading list, including books by and about women and collections that focus on the countries you want to visit. The Travelers' Tales series is a good place to start.

➤ Spend time in a specialized travel bookstore in your hometown or make an effort to visit one online. Try Book Passage (www.bookpassage.com), located near San Francisco, or the Savvy Traveler (www.thesavvytraveller.com) in Chicago. You'll be carried away by the depth of available travel titles. You can also find extensive travel collections at the Tattered Cover (www.tatteredcover.com) in Denver or Powell's (www.powells.com) in Portland.

Learn a few words in the local language—hello, good-bye, please, thank you, beautiful. If you have the time, take a language course.

◆

Marybeth Bond

➤ Seek out people who have traveled or lived in the country you'll be visiting and ask them lots of questions, especially about good reading material and whether they know citizens from there now living in the U.S.

➤ Get on the Internet and browse through the travel chat rooms and especially the news groups. You may make contact with interesting people from the country where you plan to travel. Often when you arrive you'll have a name and phone number of someone to look up.

➤ The local embassy or consulate can provide answers to general questions and will provide reading material upon request.

➤ It's easy to book a package deal—including airfare, hotel, and car rental—and there are good reasons to do so. You know you'll have no big surprises and peace of mind.

➤ Stay at a family-run guesthouse or bed-and-breakfast. Local families in many countries treat their guests like long-lost relatives. They'll cook local specialties for you, play their music, and share their evenings with you. If you join Servas (www.servas.org) you'll stay in private homes with locals who want to host you. See the Resources section for more details.

➤ Eat out at a local restaurant that serves authentic food from the country you plan to visit. Chances are that the owners or staff are expatriates and can provide valuable information.

> I never regretted any trip I took, no matter how inconvenient or expensive it seemed at the planning stage. I only regret the trips I didn't take.
>
> ◆
>
> *Marybeth Bond*

➤ Fuel your passion by planning your trip around a special interest such as art, cooking, biking, gardening, etc. If you love gardening, do targeted online research to find famous gardens you can visit at your destination, whether it is in England, India, or Japan. Contact the local tourist bureau and ask if there are historic house tours, kitchen tours, or garden tours you can take. Consider taking a cooking class in Italy, France, or Thailand. Local organizations may be able to provide helpful information about these activities at your destination. You will meet other like-minded individuals if you pursue your interests while traveling.

➤ Consider doing some volunteer work as part of your travels. Getting involved in volunteer organizations offers a great opportunity to deepen your experience and helps you get beneath the surface of a culture. See Chapter XIX for more information.

There is no age barrier to finding a new direction in life. At 65 I took my "point and shoot" camera to the Galapagos and was surprised with the results. So on my next trip—to Tibet—I took a more sophisticated camera that I knew very little about. I discovered a new career in nature photography. Age means nothing when you are doing something you love. Keeping fit is key and when you find something that moves you, like travel does, go for it.

♦

Marge Samilson, Mill Valley, California

II
PANIC AND PREPARATION

*Is there anything as horrible as starting on a trip? Once you're off,
that's all right, but the last moments are earthquake and convulsion, and
the feeling that you are a snail being pulled off your rock.*

—*Anne Morrow Lindbergh,* Gift from the Sea

EVEN THOUGH YOU MAY BE very nervous about traveling, if it
doesn't turn out to be what you expected, you can always go home.
You always have this safety net. And if you feel like there is a lot of
pressure to continue, you can simply change your plans en route.
You may decide, for example, to skip India and head straight for
Thailand. It is your trip and you make the decisions.

I give myself a pep talk: *Get
ready, things will be different where
you are traveling. Don't expect to
have as much control as you have at
home. You can expect to be uncomfortable at times, delayed often,
bored occasionally, and most cer-
tainly frustrated.* Departure is as
easy as stepping off a curb—if
you know it is there and prepare.

To prepare myself for an
upcoming trip, especially if it's to
the developing world, I make a
personal (and private) ritual to
say good-bye to my favorite com-

> Call your insurance company to
> verify that you have medical
> evacuation insurance, not just to
> the nearest hospital but all the
> way home. I was in a bus acci-
> dent in Laos and I learned the
> hard way. After weeks in a Thai
> hospital, it cost me $14,000,
> and almost my life, to get home.
>
> ◆
>
> *Alison Wright,*
> *San Francisco, California*

forts and foods at home—like my soft pillow, fresh salads, and clean
running water. I remind myself that these luxuries await me upon my
return and that I must try to be tolerant of discomfort, unfamiliar
food, and different concepts of time and personal space.

Even experienced travelers often forget that culture shock can be most intense when you return home. You may be astonished at what you see during your travels, but it is often not until your return home that shock settles in or has the room to make itself known to you. Take baths and walks, indulge yourself with the gift of time if you can. Let your digestive system readjust to what was once familiar food. Let your system integrate the experiences you've had.

When I returned from two years of travel, mostly in developing countries, my first trip to the supermarket was overwhelming. I just walked up and down the aisles, amazed at the choices. Immobilized by the bounty, unable to make any decisions, I left the store empty-handed. Common activities like driving a car or listening to my friends complain about their lives were difficult to handle. It is important to come home with an open mind to the life you left behind, because inevitably you return with a different perspective. Ease your way back into home life.

TIPS

➤ To avoid feeling over-whelmed by your impending departure, allow enough time to prepare, logistically and mentally.

➤ You will greatly reduce the stress associated with your departure if you begin pack-ing several days in advance. You will then have time to mend favorite clothes or wash dirty ones before tak-ing off.

➤ Checklists can be handy for keeping track of packing, good-byes to friends, closing

Reduce your anxiety when visiting a new country—prearrange trans-portation from the airport to your accommodations, especially if you arrive at night. Book it through a travel agent or the internet. The keyword is "transfer." It's so reas-suring to be met by a professional driver at the airport displaying a sign with your name on it. I always book a transfer for arrivals in Africa and India. The driver helps me get my luggage and work my way safe-ly through the throng of touts, beg-gars, and men offering their ser-vices as porters.

◆

Marybeth Bond

up the house, canceling the newspaper, and other necessary tasks.

➤ Take along personal photos of your friends, family, and pets. This will be a wonderful reminder of those you love.

➤ Prebook your first night's accommodation. Chances are you'll feel more comfortable in a new environment if you have a plan— where you're going (hotel, guest house, youth hostel) and how you'll get there (taxi, public transportation, rental car).

➤ Email or phone the establishment of your first night's stay, ask if they offer a shuttle from the airport. If not, what should a taxi cost? Is there a convenient, safe local bus or subway? Can they recommend a local car rental agency? (They are often less expensive than national chains.) Find answers to these questions and you'll arrive more confident and know how to proceed.

➤ Pack lightly. If you cannot carry your bag from your bedroom to the car when you are leaving, you know you will have trouble carrying it from the taxi to the lobby of your hotel or from the train platform to your train compartment. Most travelers worry about handling their luggage, so rethink what you've packed and lighten up!

➤ Traveler's insurance can cover a wide range of mishaps and emergencies, from trip cancellation, trip interruption, baggage and trip delay, and lost or stolen baggage, to rental car collision damage waiver, rental car personal accident insurance, accident medical expenses, and in-hospital indemnity. Call your insurance company to verify what their policy covers, particularly medical coverage overseas. If you have an AAA membership, you may already be covered. If you will be traveling on a shoestring, independently, or to developing countries, medical evacuation insurance is essential. Verify that your evacuation insurance covers you not just to the nearest hospital, but all the way home.

> Soon after your arrival, find a café or restaurant for what I call my "observation ritual." Sit and watch. Take specific note of the dress and behavior of women. If women don't expose their legs or arms or head, you should quickly follow suit and cover up. If they avoid eye contact, smiling, or conversations with men, be forewarned of how Western behavior may be interpreted.

> If you are traveling alone or are the least bit anxious about travel in the country of your choice, consider finding, upon arrival, a woman at the airport who is leaving the country. Ask her specific questions, such as: Is there any place that is not safe? Is there a place where Western travelers hang out and exchange information? Are there any sights, markets, or restaurants she'd highly recommend?

> To stay calm on the day of your departure, give yourself plenty of time to get to the airport, train, or bus station. Be packed and ready to go the night before.

> Be easy on yourself when you get back from a trip.

> Give yourself time to reacclimatize to your old world and make it your own again.

———— \\//// ————

We generate fears while we sit; we overcome them by action. Fear is nature's warning signal to get busy.

◆

Pacific Crest Outward Bound School, Book of Readings

III
SAFETY AND SECURITY

Use your city smarts. Try to avoid potentially dicey places like a deserted street in a big city. If you are alone, don't walk down it. Having other people around is your best safety insurance.

—*Susan Spano,* Los Angeles Times

THE MOMENT WE STEP OUT the door, we are aware of the footsteps behind us. We are concerned for our personal safety and with good reason. Safety and security are primary concerns for women, especially those traveling to unfamiliar places. To travel without fear, we need to arm ourselves with knowledge, preparedness, awareness, and a flexible attitude.

We can avoid questionable neighborhoods. We can communicate that we are self-assured by walking confidently with our heads up, aware of our surroundings. When traveling alone we can avoid countries where the men are known for hassling women, such as certain Middle Eastern countries and areas of southern Europe. If we apply the common sense we use at home, we can feel safe virtually anywhere.

>
>
> Whether traveling by bus, train, plane, or boat, try to sit next to another woman if you want to avoid potential come-ons. You may well make a new friend.
>
> ◆
>
> *Marybeth Bond*

The following tips are intended to increase your awareness, comfort level, and power to travel safely. One thing is certain: The more you travel the less fear you will experience. When in doubt, ask a lot of questions or ask for help.

If you are still concerned, tell yourself that you are a Gutsy Woman and that is, in fact, what you will become.

GENERAL SAFETY TIPS

➤ Use the common sense you've honed over the years. If you

21

wouldn't walk in an unknown neighborhood after dark at home, do not do it overseas.

➤ Trust your instincts. Let me repeat that: Trust your instincts. Instincts are not a matter of consensus. If you feel something is off, wrong, strange—get out, move on, flee, whatever is appropriate. Do it quickly.

➤ It is common for a would-be thief to use razor blades to cut purse straps, take the purse, and then get away in a thick sea of bodies. Wear a money belt to prevent this from happening.

➤ Carry all valuables, including airline or train tickets, money, passports, etc., in a money belt under your clothes. Keep only what you need for the day in your pocket or daypack.

> To ward off unwanted male attention, especially in male-dominated countries, consider wearing a fake wedding ring; make hotel reservations as if married.
>
> ◆
>
> *Marybeth Bond*

➤ If you plan on staying in hostels, carry a combination lock with you to secure your backpack to your bed or in a locker if you are leaving your room. It is also useful to attach your backpack to the luggage rack in a train compartment.

➤ It can be very difficult to know what is considered offensive or suggestive in segregated societies, such as orthodox Muslim areas. At times you may feel uncomfortable or vulnerable. You may not know if the local men view you as a sex symbol or immoral. So take your cues from the local women. Blend in. Dress appropriately. Ask other Western women who have experience in this culture for their advice.

➤ Use your judgment at public demonstrations or political rallies with massive crowds. Sometimes they can become violent and should be avoided, while other times attending such gatherings can be enlightening. If you have doubts, stay near the edge of the crowd.

➤ If you have to wait some-where, look for other women or families to sit with. If you are seated with someone, it is unlikely that you will be approached or harassed. Ask for help or company if you feel uncomfortable.

➤ If a group of men or young boys approaches you on the sidewalk, cross to the other side of the street to give them space and you peace of mind.

➤ If you are being followed on the street and you feel threat-ened, duck into a shop and firmly tell the clerk: "I am a foreigner and someone is fol-lowing me. I am frightened and need help." If need be, have the clerk call a taxi or the police for you.

➤ Always carry enough money in your shoe to get you out of a tight spot. Be willing to spend this money on a cab in order to get you to a safe

---

——— ☀ ———

Definitely take a self-defense course and never let your guard down. Then you'll feel like you can enjoy the trip.

◆

Elizabeth Harryman,
Los Angeles, California

——— ☀ ———

Alarming reports confirm an inrcease in date rape drugging. Increasingly young women in foreign countries and the U.S. have a drink with a stranger and wake up the next morning, nude, raped, and robbed. They have no recollection of what happened. Rohypnol, "the date rape drug," is odorless, taste-less, and colorless. It is a tran-quilizer that can be easily slipped into your drink. Do not accept a drink that you didn't see poured. Do not leave your glass unattended.

◆

Marybeth Bond

---

place or back to your lodging. Do not take unnecessary risks.

➤ Scam artists such as thieves and pickpockets create distractions as a cover-up. Beware of people who accidentally spill something on your clothing, bump into you, or drop a piece of luggage in front of you. This is the time to watch your luggage and keep a hand on your valuables. Don't underestimate the skill of rip-off artists—they can misdirect your attention no matter how watchful you are.

➤ Study a map before you leave your lodging or car so that once on the street you know where you are headed. Try to avoid struggling with a map or looking like a tourist.

➤ Dress moderately when you travel. Avoid wearing jewelry— even jewelry that is cheap but looks expensive.

➤ Stay alert when getting off a bus or train or riding an escalator, as this is when pickpockets tend to strike.

➤ If you must ask for directions, approach women with children or families.

> Dress conservatively. Clothing that is fashionable and appropriate at home may project a provocative image in another culture. Leave the revealing clothing at home.
>
> ◆
>
> *Marybeth Bond*

➤ Serendipity is at the heart of all travel. Once you are on the road, if you take small risks such as talking to a local person or accepting an invitation to someone's home, often your reward will be experiences you will long remember.

➤ Be sure to know when the sun sets. A bustling market can quickly empty out and be transformed into dark, deserted streets. Plan to be back to your lodging or in a safe, busy neighborhood by dark.

➤ Traveling internationally, learn how to dial for police, fire, ambulance—and your nation's consulate or embassy. Put the latter in your passport on a piece of paper with instructions in the local language explaining who to call, your blood type, any serious allergies to medicines.

ROAD TRIP SAFETY TIPS

➢ Plan your driving time during daylight hours and lock your doors when you get into your vehicle.

➢ When entering your car, be aware, look around you, and look into your car. Before you get into your vehicle, make sure no one is hiding inside.

➢ If you are parked next to a van, enter your car from the door opposite where the van is parked. Many serial killers attack their victims by pulling them into their vans.

➢ Do not enter your car if a car is parked next to it with someone sitting inside. It's always better to be safe than sorry. Do not hesitate to ask a guard or policeman to escort you to your car.

➢ As soon as you enter your automobile, lock the doors. Do not sit in a parking lot and eat, work, or sleep. This makes you a target.

➢ Restrooms at truck stops, gas stations, and public rest stops can be unsafe. Stop at moderate hotels that are likely to have a lobby, as they will usually have a clean and safe public restroom and other amenities like phones, soft drink machines, and newspaper dispensers.

➢ Crime in airport parking lots is increasing. Pay attention to where you park—look for parking spaces under lights, close to the terminal. Often the "off-airport" lots are safer. The shuttle bus picks you up at your car, takes you to the terminal, and drops you off at your car again. If it is dark and you feel uncomfortable, ask the driver to wait until you are safely inside your car.

➢ When you rent a car, ask for an up-to-date map and directions to your first meeting or hotel. Be sure to ask which neighborhoods can be dangerous and should be avoided. With the help of the rental car representative, cross off the dangerous areas on your map, so you don't accidentally drive through or stop in an unsafe area.

➤ If someone yells or honks at you, indicates that there is something wrong, or bumps your car while you are driving, do not stop. Drive to a well-lit, busy place and then check it out.

➤ If you are not already a member of the American Automobile Association (AAA), join before you take a long road trip. Their roadside assistance is invaluable.

➤ Be sure your spare tire is inflated and that you know how to change it. For added security, always carry a can of "Fix a Flat" spray in the trunk.

➤ Always carry your cell phone. Keep it close at hand, not in your purse or in the back seat. Program 911 into the automatic dial feature.

HOTEL TIPS

➤ When you check in, register using your last name and your first initial only. Also ask that your room number not be announced. If they say your room number aloud, ask to be put in another room.

➤ At check-in, request a room on the second to the sixth floors. Thieves target rooms on the ground level with easy escape access, and some fire hoses cannot reach above the sixth floor.

➤ Hang out the "Do Not Disturb" sign and leave the TV on when you leave your room. This will discourage anyone from entering your room while you are away.

➤ Always remember to carry your key with you at all times. Be careful not to leave a spare key in your room, even if it doesn't have your room number on it. If it is stolen from your room, the thief knows where to return.

➤ Always place your room key in the same location. In the event of an emergency, you will want to have time to take the key with you, allowing for your quick return if it was only a fire drill. You don't want to be caught in the hallway in a skimpy nightgown and then have to wait at the front desk for another key to be issued. Leave it on the television or on the bedside table.

➤ Carry a rubber doorstop in your luggage. This provides added security in your hotel room. Use it either on the main door or an adjoining room door that may not have double locks. Keep it in your suitcase and don't unpack it between trips.

➤ Always secure all of the locks on hotel room doors whenever you are in the room. It is essential for your protection. You could be in the bathroom and not hear someone knock. You don't want anyone to enter the room while you are inside, even to check the mini-bar or turn down your sheets.

➤ Play it safe and avoid displaying your hotel room key in public. Don't leave it on your restaurant table or on the chair by the swimming pool—it could be stolen or someone could read the name of your hotel and your room number.

➤ If someone knocks on your hotel room door, verify who it is. If there is a peephole, use it. If the person identifies him- or herself as a hotel employee, request that they come back later, when you've left the room. If they insist on entering, call the front desk and confirm that someone from the staff needs to enter your room and for what purpose before letting anyone in.

➤ If you fill out the room service breakfast order form that you hang on your door after hours, do not divulge your first name (which indicates you are female) or the number of people eating. This advertises that you are a woman and alone for the night.

➤ Request a room near the elevators and away from any renovation work. Have your key out when you leave the elevator.

➤ Lock valuables in a safe at the front desk or in your room—even while you are in the shower.

➤ If your bag is stolen from the hotel, recruit management to search for it. Most hotel robberies are committed by staff members. Many hotels do not let their staff leave with packages, so the thieves often take the money and dump the rest on the premises.

➤ When choosing a hotel, smaller is sometimes smarter: You want the staff to recognize guests and be more familiar with you. The smaller the lobby, the more noticeable loiterers become.

➤ Inquire when you book if there is sufficient staff to walk you to your room late at night. This will give you an idea of how woman-friendly the hotel is.

During one recent hotel stay, I checked into a sixth-floor room that had curtains fluttering at two open windows. I didn't think anything of it—until I woke up in the morning to see the silhouette of a man standing right behind one of them! I screamed, ran to the bathroom, and locked myself in. When I peeked out, the man was gone. I walked over to the window, looked out and realized that a fire escape was right outside. Now I always check for fire escapes when I check into a room.

♦

Janet Fullwood, Sacramento, California

IV

KEEPING IN TOUCH

*I send my words into the world and wait
for whatever new words will come.*
—*Georgia Heard,* Writing Toward Home

AFTER SAFETY, ACCORDING TO STUDIES AND POLLS conducted by hotel chains and travel publications, the second most important concern for women travelers is keeping in touch. I agree.

Depending upon where you are going and how long you are staying, keeping in touch with home may be as simple as making a phone call or sending an e-mail or text message. If you are planning a trip of a month or longer—especially in developing countries and remote areas—you'll need to prepare yourself to live comfortably without correspondence from home for periods of time.

Today, cybercafés are all over the world, from ice cream shops in San Miguel, Mexico, to local bars in small French villages. Internet access is even available in some more remote locations like northern Thailand or on the island of Tonga. Getting online is becoming less expensive and more accessible worldwide. So do not hesitate to stay in touch

Create your own travel blog so your friends and family can read about your trip as it happens. Post photos and an interactive message board. Best of all, you can't lose it, get it dirty, or spill beer on it.

◆

Marybeth Bond

with your loved ones by e-mail. It is also handy if you need to download maps or do more research on the town you are in.

TIPS

➤ Be sure to pack a copy of your address book. Do not take your original. Make a copy and paste it into an email to yourself.

➤ E-mail is often the best way to stay in touch. Check with other travelers or the desk clerk at your lodging to find the closest cybercafé.

➤ Many people still prefer communicating home by telephone. There are so many telephone company and card options now that even a simple long-distance call can be complicated. Know how to use your phone card to make long-distance calls before you leave on a trip and keep the access number for your long distance carrier in an easy-to-locate place in your address book.

➤ Avoid being overcharged by using in-room hotel phones. There are companies that now offer a callback service. Once you are registered, you simply call and enter the hotel phone number where you will be staying. At your destination, when you want to make a call, dial a special number, let it ring once, and hang up. The service will automatically call you back at your hotel (a computerized voice will ask for you by

---
—— \\\|//// ——

I began a tradition on my first trip overseas that I still practice today, sixteen years later: keeping a journal. I write as though I am penning a letter to my mother, complete with all the silly details I know she loves (like what kinds of pastries I've devoured and about my room's mismatched wallpaper). Rereading my journals is like taking a trip back in time—one much more vivid than memory alone can inspire. And for a solo traveler, it gives you something to do while you're waiting for food in restaurants.

◆

Katy Koontz, Knoxville, Tennessee

—— \\\|//// ——

When I arrived at my hotel room in Marrakech I placed a framed picture of my daughters on the bedside table. When I returned from visiting the bustling medinas later in the day, I found fresh flowers arranged around the picture. This touching ritual continued mysteriously for two days before the maid caught me in the hall, followed me to my room, picked up my picture, kissed the photo of my girls, and through gestures told me about her own family.

◆

Marybeth Bond

name). Then, once you enter your special access code, you are free to start making your calls. For now, at least, hotels don't charge for incoming calls.

➤ Give a detailed itinerary to loved ones before you leave and include your email addresses. Then ask your family or friends to email you once or twice during your trip.

➤ If your journey is going to be unstructured and spontaneous, send e-mails to keep people up to date as your plans develop, should there be an emergency at home.

➤ You can receive mail worldwide at poste restante, or general delivery, at the main post office in town. Most guidebooks can give you addresses. Your mail will be held for one month.

> ———— ⟋⟋⟋ ————
>
> Send yourself or bring home the most beautiful postcards you find. I love to display them in my office as a fond reminder of the "other me."
>
> ◆
>
> *Marybeth Bond*

➤ Advise your friends and family to address your letters clearly, avoiding cursive writing. When you go to collect mail, check under both your first and last names.

➤ To stay in touch with yourself, keep a journal.

V

HEALTH AND HYGIENE ON THE ROAD

The rewards of the journey far outweigh the risk of leaving the harbor.

—*Unknown*

———

WHEN I RETURN FROM AN EXOTIC PLACE, the first thing many people ask me is "Did you get sick?" They want to know, specifically, if I got traveler's diarrhea. Yes, that is my most common travel-related illness. To avoid it, be very careful about what you eat and drink. Eating dairy products is a hit-or-miss affair. You wouldn't want to pass up creamy pastries in Paris or gelato in Italy, but you will need to think twice before eating the same products in a developing country where refrigeration, sanitation, and pasteurization is spotty.

What about eating at food stalls? You have to take a few chances to have some wonderful culinary encounters and, yes, even risk getting sick. In Southeast Asia some of the best food available is found in the street stalls. You'll have to do some investigating, though. Ask other travelers and locals where it is safe to eat. Look for crowded places.

If you plan to travel out of the country, see your dentist prior to your trip for a complete check up. Have him or her look for loose fillings or unstable caps. Buy temporary filling material and toothache medication at the drug store. And always have one or two strong pain relief pills in your cosmetic kit. Be sure to leave them in the original prescription bottle, so customs won't ask you questions about unidentified pills.

◆

Marybeth Bond

If you plan to travel to remote areas, take along an emergency medical kit that can be used by health personnel. Include in it sterile syringes, needles, dressings, and gloves. I travel with my own individually wrapped sterile syringes. Once, after traveling for about nine months, I thought I might need another dose of gamma globulin. I was in Kathmandu at the time and although I went to a Red Cross facility, I was very pleased to hand the nurse my sterile syringe. Before my extended travels, I asked a nurse friend to prepare an official document, on her medical stationery, listing all the prescription drugs, medicines, and syringes that were in my medical kit. While I never needed this document, I was prepared for a thorough border search. Preparation and precaution will help you stay healthy.

TIPS

➢ Build up your immune system before you go by taking vitamins. You may be eating irregular meals and less nutritious food while on the road, so take along vitamins to supplement your diet.

➢ Wash your hands often and always carry antibacterial gel with you while you travel.

➢ In countries with questionable sanitation, don't drink the water. Don't brush your teeth with tap water, rinse your mouth in the shower, or put ice cubes in your drinks. Drink only bottled or treated water. Don't accept bottled water unless you see it opened in your presence. Eat only salads and fruit that you have prepared and peeled yourself.

> On a monthlong trek in the Himalayas, the most appreciated gift I shared with fellow trekkers was the use of my sunscreen and Chapstick. My lips seem to dry out and crack from the moment I step on the plane.
>
> ◆
>
> *Marybeth Bond*

➢ I swear by Pepto Bismol and Alka Seltzer tablets. I recommend you pack an ample supply.

➢ If you get diarrhea, consume fluids, eat bland, dry foods, and rest. Consider short-term use of Imodium or Ciprofloxacin. I always travel with Ciprofloxacin, which is a fabulous all-purpose antibiotic that can be used for upper respiratory problems or serious traveler's diarrhea. You'll need a prescription for it, so plan ahead. If your symptoms don't go away after self-treatment, see a doctor.

➤ Antinausea pills, such as dimenhydrinate (brand name Dramamine), are the most common over-the-counter medications used by travelers. However, side effects include drowsiness and dry mouth. For it to be effective, you must start taking it a day before your departure. If you are going on a long trip, you may want to get a prescription from your doctor for scopolamine—a thumbnail-size skin patch that you wear behind your ear.

> ____ ⋌⋌⊔⋌⋌ ____
>
> Beat Blisters! Long walks on trails or on uneven surfaces like cobblestone streets can lead to blisters. Band-aids often slip off toes and heels. Pack thin moleskin in your purse or backpack. Leave new shoes at home. Old shoes that are broken-in are the most comfortable.
>
> ◆
>
> *Marybeth Bond*

➤ Pressure point bracelets help many queasy travelers. Put them on your wrists several hours before you take off. Another form of relief is taking capsules of powdered ginger (940 mg)—available at health food stores—before a trip. I also pack candied ginger and ginger snap cookies to munch en route.

➤ For information on inoculations and all health concerns, log on to the National Centers for Disease Control and Prevention (CDC) Web site, www.cdc.gov/travel. They also have a toll-free number, 877-FYI-TRIP (877-394-8747). The CDC will give you access to important health-related travel information, including links on vaccinations and food- and water-borne illnesses.

➤ Expect the worst menstrual period of your life and don't forget a pain reliever for cramps. Take along a generous supply of tampons and panty liners.

➢ When traveling for extended periods of time and crossing multiple time zones, many women experience a temporary cessation of their periods. This can cause confusion about when to take birth control pills or if a pregnancy has begun. Carry the telephone number of your gynecologist back home and don't hesitate to call if you have a problem.

➢ In hot, humid climates, yeast infections are a common travel ailment. Taking antibiotics and wearing a wet bathing suit or tight pants, shorts, or panty hose can contribute to the infection. To avoid yeast infections, wear loose clothing that allows air to circulate. Cotton is better than silk or nylon. If you are prone to yeast infections, don't leave home without your medication.

➢ Long skirts with elastic waists are not only acceptable attire, they are comfortable in all types of weather. In heat, they allow air to circulate up your legs and thus reduce the incidence of yeast infections. They are also convenient when you encounter a squat toilet or when you have to go in the bushes.

➢ Be wary of swimming in tropical fresh water. Stagnant water can be home to snails carrying the tiny larvae that cause schistosomiasis, a dangerous disease that can

___ ⊹ ___

Getting hurt or sick while traveling may reveal fascinating aspects of the place you're visiting. On a family trip to the Philippines, I was bit by a dog. The owners of the hotel at which we were staying immediately called a local healer and before I knew it my knee was the center of a shamanic Filipino ritual involving papaya leaves, tobacco, and ancient chants. While I wouldn't recommend getting bit by an unknown animal on a remote foreign island (I did have to undergo preventive treatment for rabies upon returning to the United States), the overall experience turned out to be one of the most intriguing parts of the trip, as well as a story my family and I have told over and over.

◆

Natanya Pearlman,
Berkeley, California

damage body organs. The larvae will cause your skin to itch. Drying yourself vigorously with a towel immediately after exposure may remove most of the larvae. Before wading in, ask locals about the likelihood of such snails in the water.

➤ In developing countries it may be tempting to get an inexpensive manicure, have your ears pierced, take an acupuncture treatment, or even get a tattoo, but think twice about any activities that might puncture your skin.

➤ Cold water, ice, cold cream, or toothpaste will reduce severe itching. If in the wilderness, try using mud. If you are prone to poison oak or poison ivy, always wear long pants and be prepared with special poison ivy soap.

➤ Prevent ticks and mosquito bites by using a bug spray with high DEET content. Spray your pants, socks, and all around your ankles, neck, and back.

➤ What should be in your medical kit? See the packing list in the Resources section at the end of this book.

➤ Active travelers should pack moleskin for blisters, extra socks, comfortable shoes, sunscreen, sun hats, visors, and Vaseline to apply between toes, under bra straps, and anywhere else you might experience friction while hiking.

➤ Consider taking a travel kit of basic homeopathic remedies and a homeopathic first aid book along with your standard first aid kit. Homeopathic remedies can provide rapid, inexpensive relief from such common travel ailments as digestive problems, insect bites, rashes, sore muscles, motion sickness, and many other conditions.

➤ Pack total sunblock or a very high SPF sunscreen. It can be difficult or impossible to find high-protection sunscreens overseas. Sun, wind, water, and snow reflection can damage multiple layers of skin.

➤ If you exercise regularly at home, consider jogging in the morning on your trip. Ask hotel personnel or a local person about safety and a suggestion for a scenic route. Dress modestly in loose-fitting clothes.

➤ Do not go barefoot, especially in hostel showers. This will prevent fungal and parasitic infections as well as minimize the chance of foot cuts and injuries. Always try to keep your feet clean and dry.

➤ Avoid handling animals. Even if dogs or cats seem clean and friendly, a bite from an animal while traveling could lead to a serious disease such as rabies. You don't want to ruin your trip because of an animal bite.

➤ Always carry strong pain relief pills in your cosmetic kit—but be sure to leave them in the original bottle, so customs won't ask you questions about unidentified pills.

➤ Drink plenty of bottled water to keep yourself hydrated and healthy.

➤ When away from the comfort of your own bed, use an eye shield, wear soft silicon earplugs, or bring your pillow with you to ensure the best rest possible.

_____ ⚬ _____

I always pack my running shoes, and whenever I run, I'm rewarded with a sightseeing gem. I've jogged on mountain trails in Japan, around Tiananmen Square in Beijing, through a forest in Holland, and across San Francisco's Golden Gate Bridge. I always run in the morning to catch a glimpse of how locals greet the day.

◆

Alison Ashton,
San Diego, California

➤ Avoid all but emergency gynecological examinations and treatment in developing countries. Inadequately sterilized instruments can spread sexually transmitted diseases.

➤ Do not take chances—always use latex condoms to reduce the risk of HIV and other sexually transmitted diseases.

➤ Women can safely scuba dive during menstruation. Don't believe the stories of menstrual blood attracting sharks. Most women use tampons, which reduce blood loss to almost nothing.

➤ The U.S. National Park Service issues leaflets that advise women not to hike in bear country during their menstrual periods. Bears do pick up human scents, but no research has proven that black or grizzly bears are specifically attracted by menstruation odors. One study suggests that polar bears, which are more carnivorous than black or grizzly bears, show the same interest in the scent of menstrual blood as in the scent of seals, their natural prey. Whatever the real story, use caution when camping in bear country.

> ⎯⎯ 〰 ⎯⎯
>
> Fight microbes by washing your hands in the morning, before eating, and after visiting the bathroom. In public toilets, many people have touched everywhere you will touch, including the door handle, so use your hand sanitizer after you exit the restroom and don't rub your nose or eyes.
>
> ◆
>
> *Marybeth Bond*

➤ If you are taking oral contraceptives, you may encounter problems if you contract traveler's diarrhea or an upset stomach. Your birth control pills may not be absorbed from your intestinal tract and you may be without protection. Doctors have recommended that if you vomit within three hours of taking a pill, take another one. After severe intestinal problems your birth control pills may not be effective. Always carry a backup method of contraception if you plan to be sexually active, and take along enough to last the entire trip. Condoms are often unavailable or of poor quality in the developing world.

➤ Motor vehicle crashes are a leading cause of injury among travelers, so walk and drive defensively. Avoid travel at night, if possible, and use seatbelts when they are available.

➤ If you do get sick and need to seek professional medical services, try to find hospitals that serve the international community in major cities overseas. Call your embassy or ask the concierge at a good hotel for a reference.

AIR TRAVEL HEALTH TIPS

➤ Staying comfortable while you fly is of the utmost importance. The temperature on airplanes can vary from tropical heat to arctic chill, and you cannot always count on having a blanket provided by the airline. Dress in layers and bring a sweater. Take everything you'll need out of your carry-on bag before you stash it overhead or under the seat in front of you.

➤ Wear loose-fitting clothes. Frequent international travelers choose comfortable slacks or long skirts so they can easily cross their legs. Do not wear tight socks or nylon knee-high stockings. If they leave a mark on your leg, then they're too tight.

➤ Place your feet on top of your carry-on bags that are stowed beneath the seat in front of you. Keep them raised off the floor to increase circulation and minimize swelling.

➤ Be conscious of your posture in the plane seat. Use the pillow offered by the airline to support your lower back. Do in-seat exercises, walk around the plane, and stretch as much as possible. Be aware of posture and movement as you get up, retrieve your carry-on bag, and deplane. This is when back injuries can occur.

➤ An inflatable travel pillow for your neck is a good investment. They are inexpensive and readily available; most international airports have luggage and accessory stores that carry them. An inflatable pillow keeps the head up and prevents pulled muscles.

➤ Avoid drinks or snacks high in sodium such as Bloody or Virgin Marys, pretzels, and peanuts. Read the labels. If you consume too much salt during a long trip, your feet may swell so much you won't be able to put your shoes back on. I've seen people walk off the plane in socks, carrying their shoes!

➤ Drink a lot of water and avoid alcohol and caffeine. Eight ounces of water per hour is recommended. Not only will this keep you hydrated, it will force you to get up and use the bathroom, thus getting you up and stretching your muscles. Carry your own water bottle aboard and ask the flight attendant to fill it often. Keep it close at hand, in the seat pocket in front of you.

➤ Use an eye shield—it will keep out the light and help you fall asleep more easily and sleep more soundly. Break it in by sleeping with it once at home prior to your trip. Adjust it so that it fits snugly over your eyes, but not so tight that you perspire. A bad fit may give you a headache and will flatten your hair! Using your eye shield is also an effective way to encourage a chatty neighbor to be quiet.

➤ Pack soft earplugs to mute airplane noise, the wailing of a baby, or the rock music seeping from your neighbor's CD player. Pellet-shaped foam earplugs may do the trick, but the soft silicone (or wax) variety that conform to the contours of your ear are the most effective.

➤ Bring cloth slippers or socks in a carry-on bag. Wear them to keep your toes warm and to let your feet breathe.

➤ Consider using melatonin or a nonprescription sleeping aid such as Tylenol or Excedrin PM. Many veteran travelers claim they no longer suffer from major jet lag when they use melatonin. Take melatonin for three nights after you arrive at your destination to help you adjust to the new time zone and for three nights after you return home. Check the directions on the bottle since the dosage varies.

➤ Ever wonder why you catch a cold or the flu right after a long flight? Airlines don't introduce fresh air into the cabin as often as they used to. That means you are usually breathing recycled air with everyone else's germs. Airborne diseases are easy to contract. Savvy travelers, including many pilots and airline attendants, use a tiny portable air purifier. "Air Supply" is a battery-run air purifier about the size of a pager that is worn around your neck to help remove up to 98 percent of airborne bacteria and viruses. You can find them at local travel stores or directly at www.tenex.com.

> Air circulated through airplane cabins is extremely dry. When traveling, carry lip balm and moisturizer in your carry-on bag to help prevent chapped lips and skin. Reapply throughout your plane ride.

Melatonin has changed my life. I no longer suffer from jet lag. On either end of the trip I take 2.5 milligrams of the sublingual melatonin for three nights. I finish all my pre-bed rituals—bath or shower, vitamins, eye mask on and ear plugs in, get into bed, lights out, and then I take the pill. It's miraculous.

♦

Carol Benet, Ph.D.
Belvedere, California

> The effects of jet lag are generally more extreme when flying westbound. I use an all-natural homeopathic remedy called No Jet Lag, which is available at local health food stores, specialized travel stores, and markets like Trader Joe's.

> Try using different aromatherapy oils such as lavender, bergamot, neroli, or geranium, to help you relax during a long flight. To enliven a tired body after a flight, try essence of rosemary, clary sage, niaouli, or lemon.

> Many women experience irregular menstrual cycles because of jet lag, irregular eating and sleeping, and travel-related stress. On long flights, when long periods of sitting may aggravate premenstrual edema, try walking around the plane and exercising in your seat. Also consider reducing your salt intake the week before your period.

AIRPLANE STRETCHES

➢ Shoulder Shrug: Lift the top of your shoulders toward your ears until you feel mild tension in your shoulders and your neck. Hold your shoulders raised to your ears for five seconds, then relax and resume your normal posture. Do this two or three times every two hours.

➢ Back Twist: Interlace your fingers behind your head and raise your elbows straight out, parallel to the floor and level with your ears. Now pull your elbows backward and your shoulder blades toward one another. You'll feel a tension through your upper back and shoulder blades. Hold this position for ten seconds, then relax. Do it several times. This is a particularly good exercise to do when you've been sitting immobile and your shoulders and upper back are tense or tight.

➢ Head Roll: Begin with your head in a comfortable, aligned position. Slowly tilt your head to the left side to stretch the muscles on the side of your neck. Hold this stretch for ten to twenty seconds. You should feel a good, even stretch. Then tilt your head to the right side and stretch. Repeat this exercise two or three times on each side. Don't overdo it!

VI
THE GUTSY DINER

There are three items that can provide nourishment and energy for positive change: the air you breathe, the food you eat, and the ideas you ponder. Travel can literally import a breath of fresh air.... Eating new and different foods can nourish the spirit as well as the body.

—*Karen Page,* Becoming a Chef

————

MY MOST IMPORTANT DINING TIP is use common sense. Don't pass on the pastries in France, the pizza in Chicago, the *masala dosa* in India, or the clean food stalls in Thailand. Dining is a large part of the discovery and pleasure of travel, but it can also cause some of your worst memories.

Some people travel specifically to eat, and one of the best ways to gain an understanding of another culture is through its cuisine. The key to dining well and staying healthy is to eat the highest quality food possible. Only you can decide how bold you'll be, but it's part of the adventure of travel to try new things.

I may consider myself a risk taker, but when it comes to the equilibrium of my stomach, I am extremely cautious. Well, I did eat bamboo grubs in northern Thailand and yak eyeballs in Tibet, but both times they were well cooked and gave me less grief than eating a fast food hamburger in the USA. There are some gastronomic opportunities you just can't pass up!

Bon appétit!

————

I make a deal with myself. I can try anything that I have never tasted before. I already know what chocolate, tiramisu, pâté, prime rib, smoked salmon, etc. taste like. Foods that I've never tried before and probably won't have the opportunity to sample at home are worth the exception. I give myself permission to enjoy them wholeheartedly. Everything tastes better without guilt.

◆

Laurie Armstrong,
San Francisco, California

43

TIPS

➤ Eat only thoroughly cooked food or fruits and vegetables you have peeled yourself. Remember: boil it, cook it, peel it—or forget it.

➤ Look at your meal carefully before you take the first bite. Never eat undercooked beef, pork, lamb, or poultry or raw eggs. Raw shellfish can be particularly dangerous to individuals who have liver disease or compromised immune systems.

➤ Do not eat or drink dairy products unless you know they have been pasteurized.

➤ Don't let yourself get dehydrated. Always carry a bottle of water with you when you travel and be sure to drink from it throughout the day. Do not wait for your body to tell you that you are thirsty—replenish continually.

> _I relax my vegetarianism when I travel. It's much easier to make friends when I'm not trying to explain that I can't eat the foods they've kindly offered me._
>
> ♦
>
> _Jill Robinson,_
> _Mill Valley, California_

➤ Always carry a snack with you—you never know when you will need a little nourishment. Your growling stomach may wake you up in the middle of the night in a hotel with no room service or you could be stuck at a train station where everything is closed. Be prepared to nourish yourself immediately with nuts, dried fruit, or an energy bar.

➤ If you find yourself in a hole-in-the-wall restaurant where English is neither written nor spoken, just gesture to the waiter to follow you and walk right into the kitchen. Start pointing to this or that and make motions about how you want things cooked. The staff will love it. Ham it up. It is a great way to have a terrific meal and make friends.

➤ When dining at food stalls, be sure the meat is well cooked or the soup has been boiling for a while. Many of my seasoned travel friends say they wouldn't miss eating the mouth-watering local specialties available, at very reasonable prices, at food stalls. Others never go near them. As for me, I size up the cleanliness of a stall, the clientele, the vendor, the

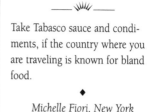

Take Tabasco sauce and condiments, if the country where you are traveling is known for bland food.

◆

Michelle Fiori, New York

food offered, and how it is cooked. I have had many fabulous meals and only a few painful memories from food stall experiences.

➤ Take along herbal tea. In many countries there are no decaffeinated beverages available.

➤ There is protocol for eating with your hands that must be learned from the local people, as it varies from country to country. Watch how the locals eat and ask if there is a certain etiquette.

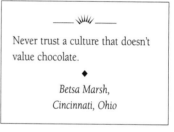

Never trust a culture that doesn't value chocolate.

◆

Betsa Marsh,
Cincinnati, Ohio

For example, in Malaysia it is considered bad manners if the food touches your hand too far up your finger, past the second knuckle. When in India, eat only using your right hand. The left hand is used for bodily hygiene and considered unclean.

➤ You will encounter different cultural challenges when dining on the road. A few you will want to remember:

Don't be surprised if you are a guest in a Muslim home and the hostess does not join you for dinner. Muslim women eat separately from the men.

If you are a guest out to dinner in Hong Kong, you can offer to pay even though it will probably not be accepted. Do not offer to split the bill, as this will result in loss of face for your host.

In Singapore, if you want to ensure good fortune, always make sure there is an even number of people present at the table.

In Taiwan, do not place your chopsticks parallel on top of your bowl or standing straight. This is bad luck and considered synonymous with a funereal ritual and death.

➢ Do not be afraid to eat by yourself in a restaurant. When choosing a restaurant, select one that appeals to your senses and mood. Do you feel like meeting other travelers? Select a lively bistro or café where you can sit at a counter or where the tables are close together. If you are in the mood to be alone, choose a restaurant that is quiet, where you sense you will not be bothered.

➢ If dining alone, why not ask to be seated at the counter or near the kitchen? You can pick up a number of tips while watching the staff or chef at work. Check out the growing number of restaurants that offer a counter where you can cozy up to the kitchen and personally interact with a celebrity chef.

_____ ⚶ _____

You'll always remember the lavish dinner at a highly rated, upscale restaurant at your vacation destination—if for no other reason than the price. But picnics are another way to create indelible dining memories, and they stretch your travel budget at the same time. My travels have led me to memory-making picnics. On an unusually warm spring day, my husband, Jack, and I headed for the ruins of an ancient temple and theater in Sicily. There couldn't have been a more elegant setting for our simple lunch of crusty bread, salty prosciutto, cheese, sharp olives, and sparkling mineral water. Was our picnic inconsequential when compared to the breathtaking scenery? Not at all—it was a perfect complement, giving us a chance to linger and drink more deeply of the magnificent ancient theater.

◆

Marcia Schnedler,
Little Rock, Arkansas

➤ Dining alone is an acquired skill. Take a book, postcards, or stationery with you so that you can enjoy your time in the restaurant.

➤ Ask your hotel concierge about restaurants that offer communal dining. From a small table of four to a large table of thirty, you never know with whom you will be seated. It is an opportunity to connect with other people—locals and travelers.

Don't pass up the opportunity to eat fabulous street food. Select a crowded, clean-looking stall. In Bali or Bangkok you may find everything from crickets to fried ants and snakes. Savor the initial "crunch." Remember, the story will be worth it when you get home.

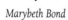

◆

Marybeth Bond

VII

ROMANCE ON THE ROAD

We travel, some of us forever, to seek other states, other lives, other souls.

—*Anaïs Nin, The Diary of Anaïs Nin*

THERE IS SOMETHING extremely romantic about travel. The change of scenery often prompts you to step outside yourself and expand your normal boundaries. Maybe at home you wouldn't talk to a strange man or woman you met in a café and then later meet them for dinner. But when traveling, general rules are often pushed aside and new adventures take place. Wonderful things can happen when you meet exotic foreigners or other travelers. Only you can decide when or if to indulge in romance on the road. You could meet the love of your life, man or woman. I met my husband in the Kathmandu Guesthouse in Nepal, and some of my friends have also met their spouses or significant others while traveling. Or they've had incredible experiences that they place very close to their heart. Keep in mind, though, that the chances of an on-the-road romance continuing once you return home are not great. It's very difficult to keep a

If it hadn't been for my incurable wanderlust, I never would have met my husband. If it hadn't been for the gentle charms of the Caribbean, I'd probably still be single. It is a wonderful story with a moral most profound. Sometimes you have to listen to your heart and not your head. The very things that attracted me to Bill for a shipboard romance were what seemed to make him unsuitable as a permanent mate. China blue eyes, sun-blond hair, an over-all tan, and a nomadic lifestyle? Hardly the stuff on which to base anything long-term, I kept telling myself. Thankfully, Bill was smarter about relationships than I.

◆

Judy Wade,
Phoenix, Arizona

long-distance romance alive, but you never know when or where you'll meet your soulmate.

I always encourage you to meet new people in public spaces. Be sure you know what the other person's intentions are, and also be clear about what you want out of the interaction. If you are interested in a short fling while traveling, be smart.

Gutsy Women, if you are open to love and romance on the road, always remember to be safe.

My philosophy has always been: Do what you love, follow your passion, and romance will follow. It has worked for me.

◆

Marybeth Bond

TIPS

➢ If you want to meet a like-minded companion or partner, participate in an organized tour with a special focus that appeals to you, such as an archeological dig, a lesbian cruise, or an opera tour.

➢ Health spa retreats or meditation centers are good places to meet potential partners. People go to these places when they are making a life change and they are often more open and friendly. There is a time for group sharing and you talk about why you are there and what is going on in your life. Most people attend these sessions alone.

➢ Always watch your beverages while you are in a bar or restaurant to prevent tampering. The "date rape" drug, rohypnol (or roofie), may look as innocent as aspirin but is actually a very dangerous narcotic. A potent tranquilizer similar in nature to Valium, but many times stronger, rohypnol produces a sedative effect, amnesia, muscle relaxation, and a slowing of psychomotor responses. Sedation occurs within twenty-to-thirty minutes. Go to bars with a buddy and keep an eye on each other.

➢ Be clear about what you want so you don't give mixed signals. If you want a fling, enjoy it. If you want something more lasting, examine your own feelings and ask yourself if his interest is genuine. Imagine introducing this person to friends and loved ones at home. Then trust your instincts.

➤ If you are the least bit inclined to find a lover, pack a supply of condoms. Remember, condoms bought in Bulgaria or India are not likely to be of the same quality as those bought at home. Some men, in many areas of the world, are not accustomed to discussing contraception and have negative feelings about using condoms, but you should insist on using them nonetheless.

Make smart choices and use your common sense. Don't be paranoid, but be aware that bad things do happen, and protect yourself. In some countries accepting one or more drinks from an unknown man indicates your acceptance to sleep with him. Make your intentions clear.

♦

Marybeth Bond

➤ If you are a lesbian, you may be able to identify easily who is gay in your own culture. It is not so easy in other cultures. Try to learn the cultural attitudes toward gay people in the country you are visiting before you begin to flirt.

➤ In numerous countries, such as Pakistan, Morocco, and India, upscale hotels and tourist offices can arrange for a reliable male escort. He acts as your guide and bodyguard. This is not a cop-out. In some Muslim areas it is worth the minimal investment to enjoy touring without continual harassment.

➤ To avoid unwanted advances, there are several things you can do:

Dress conservatively and communicate an air of confidence and respectability.

Walk with purpose.

Think and look ahead to anticipate compromising situations.

Consider wearing a wedding ring, if you don't already.

Try to sit or stand next to other women or family groups in restaurants, on trains or buses, and in other public places.

➤ If you begin to get pestered:

Completely ignore comments, catcalls, and whistles.

Avoid all eye contact.

Don't try to speak their language—or instead, learn, "Please leave me alone" in the local language and say forcefully.

Listen to your inner voice. If you are uncomfortable, get out of the situation immediately.

If you do have a one-night fling, be careful not to expose your money to that person. This happened to me: I got up and went to the bathroom. In the morning, after he was gone, I discovered he had stolen all the cash out of my purse. You never know who you can trust, especially if it is a guy you'll never see again.

◆

Anonymous

A friend told me that when she goes to work out in the fitness center of her hotel, she spends all of her time in the free-weight section. Most women gravitate to the aerobics classes and the exercise machines, so she is often the only woman in an area filled with men and there is lots of good flirting.

◆

Judith Babcock Wylie,
Santa Cruz, California

➤ If the pestering turns nasty, use forceful resistance: scream, fight, and flee! Research shows that rapists often seek to feel power and control over a weaker person. Your best defense is to resist and flee.

➤ In crowded environments like buses, men may harass you by pressing themselves against you. Don't let them get away with it. If the advance is especially ugly—suppose he presses his genitals against you—plant your elbow in his mouth, then scream at him (not swearing) in English with an air of great indignation.

➤ There is power in vocal embarrassment. I have found that many men are shamed by a verbal, loud woman admonishing them in public. Also shame them by shaking your finger in their faces. Even if the crowd doesn't understand your words, they will understand your indignation and gestures. Most sleazy men do not want public attention.

I was free and single when I was traveling so my experiences of foreign cultures were sometimes enhanced by my encounters with foreign men. I considered myself fairly sophisticated and savvy, but in retrospect I was rather naïve about my involvements—or maybe I was just hopelessly romantic. My adventures tended to obscure the reality that, as a Western woman, I've come to expect a certain level of respect and attentiveness that often wasn't granted by men of non-Western cultures. Ultimately, I realized (after many heartaches and disappointments) that I could never get what I needed from a relationship that sprang from fantasy to begin with.

◆

Kennerly Clay, Philadelphia, Pennsylvania

VIII
BUDGET AND MONEY MATTERS

Take half the clothes and twice the money.
—*Marybeth Bond*

———

ALTHOUGH I HAVE BEEN ASKED dozens of times what it cost me to travel around the world for a year, it is almost impossible for me to say what it will cost *you* to stay for a month in Asia or two weeks in Europe. What you will spend depends on where you stay, where and what you eat, how you travel (plane, train, bus, rental car, on foot or bike), and how fast you travel. One person who travels twice as fast as another will spend a great deal more. Transportation, transfers in and out of cities, and lodging are a large percentage of a budget. A week lying on the beach in southern Thailand watching the waves roll in brings down your daily costs. If you stay in luxury hotels, fly everywhere, or see a lot of countries in a very short time you can spend a lot of money.

I spent under $5,000 to travel for a year, spending most of that time in Southeast Asia. That included all of my airfare, food, gifts, communications home—everything. Perhaps I could have spent half this amount, but I didn't want to scrimp and stay in dormitories or the cheapest hotels, always travel second class on trains, and learn to exist on rice and tea. I splurged to fly to Sri Lanka and the Maldives (where I went scuba diving...talk about expensive), and I enjoyed the old-fashioned Raj-style luxury of India's charming Maharaja Palace hotels. Remember that, most times, you will get what you pay for and many times its worth in unique experiences by paying a little more.

If you are traveling independently and are not going to one location (such as a condo in Hawaii), the best way to figure out a budget for yourself is to buy a good guidebook and study it. Spend some time in a specialized travel bookstore sifting through the guides available for your destination. You can learn a great deal about the average prices for lodging, food, transportation, and entertainment in this way.

Unless you have a generous budget for your travels, choose your activities and countries carefully. Many areas of Asia (Nepal, India, Indonesia, Thailand, parts of China) and South America (Peru, Ecuador) are not only inexpensive areas to travel, they are also very welcoming to women. The longer you are gone from home, the lower your per diem will be. If you have the time, plan on staying in one area for a week or more. You will meet more local people as well as experienced travelers and learn where to eat, what to do, and where to stay. When I traveled around the world I focused on remote areas where I knew I could not go on a short corporate vacation. I discovered that the longer I was gone, the less I spent.

My well-kept secret for taking a very inexpensive getaway trip is to go somewhere, by myself or with a friend, and stay in a hostel. They have kitchens and dining rooms and common rooms. In the evenings there is a great mix of people from around the world. Most of them are under thirty, but there are some "boomers" and "seniors." You basically walk into an instant dinner party with interesting international guests.

♦

Cathy Beaham,
Kansas City, Missouri

TIPS

➤ Budget killers include not shopping around for your plane tickets; calling home too often; using taxis excessively; eating out all the time; staying at international chain hotels. When in doubt, ask other travelers (before and during your trip) for their budget, lodging, and restaurant tips.

➤ You can save a lot of money by planning in advance. Consider alternative accommodations. For example, if you have done your research about Ireland, you will have learned about all the bed-and-breakfasts in the country. Not only are they much less expensive than staying in a hotel, they offer a huge breakfast, warm hospitality, and a chance to meet the people, not just see the sights. I have stayed in bed-and-breakfasts in the USA (even in Los Angeles!) to cut costs and add charm and intimacy to my travels.

➤ Vary your travel. Try second class some of the time. Cut your transportation costs by traveling the way locals do.

➤ Ask the locals where they eat out. Leave the tourist areas of a city to find less expensive restaurants in more residential neighborhoods.

➤ Don't buy a whole new wardrobe for your trip prior to departure. Keep your pre-trip shopping to a minimum. Buy what you need as you travel.

I travel with a debit card, and two credit cards: Visa or MasterCard. It is cheaper and easier to use a debit card to get cash than to hassle with traveler's checks and you get the best bank exchange rate. When you use a debit card you are typically charged a lower transaction fee than if you use your credit card. Contact your credit and debit card companies before you leave to notify them of the countries you will be visiting. They will make a note of where you'll be using your cards to charge and draw money from your account. Banks will close an account if they see a lot of activity in a foreign country and don't have prior information about your travel plans. It happened to me in Budapest and it was a big hassle to open my account again.

◆

Marybeth Bond

➤ Negotiate the price of your hotel room. If you've got the guts, why not try? You must call the hotel directly; do not use the central 800 number. Decide how much you can spend, wait until late in the day, and speak to the hotel manager. Tell him what you can spend. Hotel rooms are a perishable item. Often they will accommodate you. Your chances of getting a lower rate for a room are better on the weekend in the city and during the week outside major cities.

➤ When making reservations for car rental, accommodations, or miscellaneous tickets, always mention your membership in an organization—the American Association of Retired Persons (AARP), AAA—or affiliation to an academic institution. Often discounts are available for the asking.

➤ For airline tickets, car rentals, and hotel rooms, always ask, "Is this the lowest rate available today?"

➤ If you are staying at an establishment for a long time, or will be returning often, meet with the management and negotiate a special rate.

➤ Travel with a pocket calculator. I use it to help me figure out the exchange rate until I've worked out a simple formula. I use it to calculate the approximate amount of a credit card charge (in U.S. dollars), which I write at the bottom of each receipt.

➤ Make a double-sided photocopy of your credit cards, ATM card, passport, and eyeglass or contact lens prescription to carry in your money belt.

> ———— ⚜ ————
>
> Keep $20 in small bills tucked away at all times. You may be leaving a country and find out there is a departure tax or if you need a tip upon arriving in a new country. This will save you from having to stand in line to get local currency at inconvenient and often stressful departure and arrival times.
>
> ◆
>
> *Marybeth Bond*

➤ Play purchasing exercises with yourself while window-shopping to build your sense of the local currency—when you are ready to step into the store or stall, you will be better prepared to bargain. Memorize a currency "ladder" if you find it helps, e.g., how many rupees constitute $5, $10, $50? If you have a spending limit for a certain item, keep that number in mind in the foreign currency, not just in dollars.

➤ Protect your valuables. All of your important documents and money should be worn on your body. Buy a comfortable money belt or neck pouch. When the shoeshine boy and his buddies robbed a friend in Rio, they snatched the bills he took out of his trouser pocket and ran. They got $14. He had another $50 inside his sock and clothing. Only pull out small amounts of money at a time.

➤ Consider staying in a youth hostel. They are safe, friendly, people-oriented places filled with other budget-minded, adventurous travelers. There are over 5,000 hostels in 70 countries, including 150 in the USA. Not only do hostels offer extensive information about what to do locally, you will meet people who have already been where you may want to go and can give you the inside scoop on the good places to see, eat, and shop. Some hostels offer bicycle, canoe, or kayak rentals.

━━━ ⚘ ━━━

For the past decade, my friend Renae and I have left husband (hers), children (hers and mine), and, most recently, our grandchildren at home for destinations overseas. This past spring, our plans were to see how inexpensively we could travel in England and Scotland and at the same time do everything that excites us: go to the theater, see old friends, find the finest gardens, visit museums and art galleries. We wondered, as well, just how flexible and adaptable we really were, how well we'd cope with the unknown. So both of us decided that nothing less than staying at youth hostels would do. On the cheap, we concurred, is not just for the young! Would we do it again? Yes!

◆

Rachel Pollack, Denver, Colorado

➤ These days YMCAs aren't just for young Christian men! There are branches in many major cities throughout the world, such as Hong Kong and New Delhi, that are safe and well located. You can make a reservation with a phone call and a credit card. If you don't like the accommodations or location, you can move after the first night. Be careful that the facility is not located in an unsafe neighborhood.

➤ If you travel in and out of major cities, use ATM withdrawals and credit card advances. If you'll be in remote areas for long periods of time, consider traveler's checks and some cash.

➤ The best exchange rate you will find is through ATMs because they provide local currency (debiting your bank account at home). They give you the wholesale exchange rate and this can be from 5 to 10 percent higher than you get at hotels or exchange offices! Check with your bank about how to access your account overseas.

➤ When traveling internationally, it is recommended that your credit or debit PIN be four digits long. If your PIN is longer than four digits, consider contacting your financial institution and ask them to issue you a new PIN number. If you have an alphabetic PIN, translate the letters into numbers before leaving the country.

——— 〜⑊⑉⁄ ———

When traveling to developing countries, make sure that your bills are crisp and clean. Twice, once in Africa and once in Asia, banks refused to take my large bills because they had ink marks and they were dirty. Many shopkeepers will also refuse soiled or marked bills.

◆

Marybeth Bond

➤ Guard your PINs carefully, whether they are for your ATM card or your telephone credit card. Stand close to the phone when dialing and punching in your number. Phone card thieves work public places with binoculars.

➤ Financial institutions may have restrictions on daily withdrawals that apply even when you are in another country. Check with your bank to find out how much you can take out each day.

➤ Before returning to the USA, convert all of your foreign coins and bills into U.S. dollars at the airport. Banks and exchange offices in the U.S. only accept bills and charge a hefty fee. Last summer I returned from Canada with $10 in Canadian bills. The fee to convert them to U.S. currency was $5. If you plan to return to that country again soon, you may be better off just holding on to the currency.

_____ ⚜ _____

Be cautious when you buy an airline ticket from a consolidator or "bucket shop." Make sure they're legal and legitimate. Ask to speak to a past customer. Pay by credit card, which allows you to stop payment if your tickets don't materialize.

◆

Marybeth Bond

IX
BARGAINING AND TIPPING

Bargaining is a game around the world—a game of wit and skill and words. Bring your best poker face, and prepare for fearless entertainment.
—*Kathy Borrus, The Fearless Shopper*

I LOVE TO WANDER through bazaars and markets looking for local handicrafts when traveling. I use different negotiating styles with different vendors, rickshaw drivers, or cabbies and in different situations. Some travelers find bargaining humiliating, while others revel in it. It can be an unexpected source of local information and even friendship. When I find haggling with street vendors degrading, I give in or don't buy. I am rarely on a budget so tight that I can't spend an extra dollar or two.

Once I fell in love with a beautiful jade disk necklace in the old town in Hanoi. I saw it in the glass cases of several shops before I asked the price and began to compare the workmanship on the hand-tooled silver casing. When I finally found a shop with several nice ones, I began to bargain. From the very beginning, I should have realized I had met my match, laughed, and given up. But I didn't. The Vietnamese woman, about my age, grew tired of my negotiating. She

In the United States, you're a person as much as you are a woman; in most of the world, you learn that you are only a woman—until you pull out your credit card.

♦

Joan Medhurst,
Alameda, California

appealed to my husband and to our guide, and finally, with an air of indignation after my last offer, she bellowed, "Lady you cheap!" It is a funny story to tell now but, at the time, I was humiliated. I paid her asking price and hurried off. In the end, we were both losers, because I was planning to buy three necklaces instead of one. I smile and think of her every time I wear my "Lady You Cheap" necklace. She taught me an important lesson—pay the higher price and get what you want.

A friend of mine once bargained for a set of silver pony bells in a Tibetan town, but the old man offering them was absolutely unyielding in his price: $50 U.S. This seemed very high given the other goods and prices being offered at the market, and so my friend went home without the bells. Eight years later he reports that every Christmas he thinks wistfully of those bells as he puts up decorations. He realized that the bells may well have had a history for the old man, who was reluctant to part with them unless he got a very good price. Remember that the worth of something lies not in what is paid for the item, but what it means in your heart and life.

BARGAINING TIPS

➤ Before you begin bargaining, decide if you really want to buy the item. Do not waste your time or the salesperson's.

➤ Decide the top price you are willing to pay and know what that amount is in the local currency. Travel with a pocket calculator and use it to figure out the exchange rate before you pass through the doors of temptation.

➤ Eye contact with a shopkeeper will lead to a conversation. If you look them in the eyes, it can lead to a string of questions and it may be difficult to extricate yourself from the conversation without feeling rude.

➤ Do not be taken in by engaging come-ons, such as this summons by a leather merchant in Antalya, Turkey, "Madame, I have everything you want." Shopkeepers can be humorous and talented manipulators and will play on your sense of politeness. Only enter stores that you want to, and walk by those that you do not wish to enter—no matter how much the salesperson chides you.

➤ Occasionally accept offers of hospitality. I sipped a hot cup of apple tea in a spice market in Marmaris, Turkey, and heard all about a merchant's family and spice business. I did purchase spices from him, and even if I overpaid a little, it was worth it because I have the memory of the time spent with him in his shop.

➢ Don't ask the price right away. In fact, look disinterested in the item you would like to buy. When you ask the price, if it is above what you had decided you would pay for such an item, leave. After this tactic, the merchant will usually approach you with a better price. Let the bargaining begin!

Many people will ask you for money. Try to avoid giving money, especially to beggars on the street. In developing countries, they are often professionals. Be careful whom you give to. Not only will you burn out if you are cheated, but you may turn proud people into beggars. You will often know when people really need it.

♦

Olga Murray, Sausalito, California

➢ Don't rush a good negotiation. Chat and have fun with it. Remember, it's all a dance and you will know when you are comfortable buying the item or walking away.

➢ Bargaining will vary from country to country. In India, for example, the first counteroffer can be 40 percent of the asking price and hopefully you can meet in the middle. In Turkey, however, you may only bargain for a ten or fifteen percent reduction. Ask the hotel manager, taxi driver, tour guide, or a local what they consider the local bargaining rules to be.

➢ Communicate shipping and payment arrangements early in the negotiations. If you are paying by credit card, the price may be higher. If you pay in cash, see what kind of discount this will add. If shipping an item, make sure that you agree upon shipping method and time frame.

➢ If you are interested in buying more than one item, use that information as a bargaining tool for a larger discount.

➤ If you can afford the item, don't haggle over pennies or even dollars. Consider the merchant's lifestyle. The extra income could make a big difference in his or her life—if it won't impact your own, then pay a little more.

➤ Even if you end up not purchasing an item you have been bargaining for, be pleasant and leave the merchant on good terms.

Enjoy your new purchase and the relationship you made with the merchant. Don't look at the price of the same item later in the market, as it may only upset you. Be happy with the item and the experience.

♦

Marybeth Bond

➤ Contrary to popular wisdom, duty-free shops are not always filled with bargains. International passengers do not have to pay local taxes since they are exiting the country with the items, but sometimes merchants mark up prices to take advantage of a captive audience. If you have done your research and know what you are looking for, then there are bargains to be had.

TIPPING GUIDELINES

➤ There is no worldwide standard for tipping for services, but here is my rule of thumb: Never tip less than the price of a beer in the local currency.

➤ What might be viewed as a discretionary tip in our culture may be a necessary bribe for basic services in another. For example, in India tipping is a way of getting things accomplished. I have discovered that in some countries you must tip restroom attendants to receive a paper towel or toilet paper. If you don't tip them, they may follow you with a stream of insults.

➤ In addition to giving a monetary tip to someone like your guide, with whom you have spent several days, add something that will be meaningful to him or her. After climbing Mount

Kilimanjaro, my husband and I tipped our guide in cash and gave him our daypack. He was absolutely overjoyed with it because such packs were unavailable in Tanzania.

➤ If a taxi does not have a working meter, or the driver won't use one, avoid hassles or misunderstandings at the end of your taxi journey by negotiating the fare prior to entering the cab. Have a piece of paper available and insist he write the amount on it. Then be prepared for him to make one last effort for more money before you get out.

If you don't bargain, what is the worst thing that can happen? You might pay a little more than you would have if you'd haggled; a merchant in a developing country you don't know will gloat over hoodwinking a naïve tourist—but you'll end up with the object you wanted to have and maintain a mood you also wanted to keep.

◆

Claire Walter, Boulder, Colorado

➤ In some cultures tipping is not customary or recommended. In Singapore it is officially discouraged and in Japan it is virtually unknown. In other cultures the service charge or gratuity is included in every bill. Ask a local person about the tipping customs of the country you are visiting.

➤ If tips are automatically included in a bill it is not necessary to leave more, but it may be customary to leave a small amount in cash. For example, in good Parisian restaurants the French leave an additional 5 percent on the table.

➤ Be careful when you sign your credit card charge form. Most receipts have a separate box for the gratuity. If there is no tip box on the form, ask the waiter how to include it in the charge.

➤ Some unscrupulous restaurant personnel have been known to write the total amount of the bill, including a predetermined tip and service charge, in the top box of the charge slip. They leave the "tip" and "total" boxes empty and fill in an additional tip and new total after you have signed the bill. Ask if the tip is included and if it is, rewrite the total at the bottom before signing.

➤ Make sure to thank flight attendants who give you good service. They have a tough job and aren't paid well these days, nor are they allowed to accept tips. But a smile and a "thank you" can mean a lot.

X
COMFORT ON THE ROAD

Up in the air you breathed easily, drawing in a vital assurance and lightness of heart. In the highlands you woke up in the morning and thought: Here I am, where I ought to be.

—*Isak Dinesen,* Out of Africa

WHEN I'M TRAVELING, there are always little things I do to remind myself of home. I have heard numerous stories of the various ways women create rituals to help them relax or find a little bit of home on the road. Whether you are stressed out because of transportation hassles—airline delays, cancelled flights, missed trains—or you need a way to get back in touch with yourself when you are feeling swept away, rituals are simply something that you do to feel comfortable and more in control.

When you travel, there are many times when you may need a ritual to reduce stress and clear a way for you to enjoy your destination. Maybe you are on a business trip and you simply need to do something that will make you feel like you have a life outside of work. The following rituals are small things you can do to retreat from your travel life and focus on yourself.

I'm sure if you begin to think about it, you will realize that you do have a few rituals that you practice on the road. I encourage you to consider the following and invent your own. It's important to take care of yourself while you travel. Next time you travel and are feeling frustrated or overwhelmed, breathe deeply and try one of the following exercises.

RITUALS

➤ Start every day with a good breakfast, exercise (even if you only stretch or walk for fifteen minutes), and drink plenty of water to prevent dehydration and periods of afternoon low energy.

➤ Put on comfortable clothes and stretch. Start with your neck and work your way through your whole body.

➤ Light a candle and meditate. Focus on your breath and empty your mind of all of the thoughts that are racing around. This will enhance your pleasure of what's to come.

➤ Take a long bath. Bring bubble bath and candles from home to make it special. If you don't have any accessories, simply relax in a warm tub.

➤ Listen to music.

➤ Take a shower and stand still for a minute to feel the warm water trickling from your head down to your toes. Imagine your discomfort and tension being washed away, leaving you cleansed and refreshed.

➤ Leave your lodging and find somewhere outdoors to sit. Wander through a park, watch the locals from afar, or stare at the moon. Just be still and let the world pass around you.

➤ Practice reflexology. Give your ear a massage and it will be like you had a full body message. There are over a hundred reflexology energy points located in your ears that are connected to different organs and body parts.

➤ Wake up the Chinese way. Practice tai chi, an ancient martial art form. If you are lucky enough to be in Hong Kong, contact the Hong Kong Tourist Association for free lessons—in English—

———— ⚡ ————

While traveling, I set aside time each day to write in my journal. What are five new things I saw today? Whom did I meet? How do I feel? It slows me down to notice the details of my journey, so I can savor the people, the sights, the food, my inner landscape. It helps me realize that my travels are not just about viewing the world, they're about truly seeing myself.

◆

Lisa Bach, Oakland, California

three mornings a week in the Garden Plaza, Hong Kong Park (800-282-4582).

➤ Read a good book. Bring along a couple of paperbacks to read along the way. When you finish one, exchange it with another traveler.

➤ Make a scrapbook as you travel. All the ticket stubs, brochures, maps, and other things you pick up in your travels make ideal material for your scrapbook. If you take a scrapbook, a pair of scissors, and a glue stick with you on your trip, the ten minutes you spend each night on your scrapbook will make it a treasured item. Otherwise, you might end up with a bag of miscellaneous items that never make it into a book because you are not quite sure what they are or where you collected them.

MAKE YOUR HOTEL ROOM
A HOME AWAY FROM HOME

So many people complain about their hotel rooms—why not make improvements to them instead? Even if you are only staying for a couple of nights, try to make it feel as much like home as possible.

➤ Unpack your suitcases and put them away. Do not live out of the suitcases. If you are used to having a sock and underwear drawer, then unpack and create the same organization.

➤ Place a framed photo of your family or friends on the bedside table.

➤ If you are used to having flowers in your home, go to a local florist and get yourself a small bouquet to keep in your room. Or keep the flower from a room-service cart for your room.

➤ Move the desk to where it is most comfortable for you to work. If you like to have a view or more natural sunlight when you read or write, move the desk near the window.

➤ When you buy presents for friends and family, have them gift-wrapped with a pretty ribbon. Leave these gifts out in your hotel room for a festive look and a connection to home.

➤ Hide all of the hotel's promotional reading material and place your magazines or books in their place.

When all else fails, throw money at it. If you're delayed three hours at an airport, don't fret in the crowded waiting area, find the best restaurant and splurge on a good meal.

◆

Scottie Held, Bolton, Massachusetts

XI

THE BUSINESS TRAVELER

Enjoy the place you are visiting. Don't work all the time.

—Anonymous Frequent Flyer

GUTSY BUSINESSWOMEN—we're everywhere: on airplanes, checking into hotels, renting cars, giving speeches, talking on cell phones, and making important deals all over the world. Business travel is an essential part of modern corporate life, and in the next few years over 50 percent of all business travelers will be women.

Travel is a wonderful perk for many working women, although after the first few trips many individuals do not find it fun or glamorous anymore. It adds stress and consumes personal time we might rather spend with friends and family. Can we learn ways to be smart business travelers? Frequent flyers whose jobs demand that they travel will tell you "Yes." They live on airplanes, at airports, in hotels, driving countless miles in rental cars.

Here are some basic, road-tested tips to help make your business travel easier.

> ___ ⋰⋰⋰ ___
>
> Always travel with a Pashmina shawl, it can be used as a coat, a sweater, a scarf, a pillow, a belt, or even a beach cover-up.
>
> ◆
>
> *Gail Krauss,*
> *Vermilion, Ohio*

TIPS

➤ Record all of your confirmation numbers—hotel, car rental, flight information, etc.—in your calendar, Palm Pilot, or journal. I have jotted down these vital numbers on my airline ticket jacket and later discovered that an efficient ticket agent threw it away and gave me a clean one. If your reservation is lost or the computer is down, you will be prepared. If your flights are delayed, you'll need to call ahead to confirm a late arrival; if you bring the vital phone and confirmation numbers with you, handling the situation will be a breeze.

I have a cosmetic bag prepacked with travel size items that I know I always need when I'm traveling for business. I never have to worry about getting somewhere and not having a toothbrush, toothpaste, shampoo, conditioner, Q-tips, deodorant, etc. It's a great relief to simply grab the kit and go.

♦

Kim Arnone, Berkeley, California

➤ Pack lightly, bringing only carry-on luggage if possible. Pack the least amount of clothes you think you can survive on. You can wear the same mix-and-match outfits day after day. Leave room in your bag for shopping treasures you can't resist along the way.

➤ How many shoes does the gutsy business traveler pack? Too many, usually! If the shoe fits, wear it, don't carry it. Wear the shoes you'll need for business and pack one pair of athletic shoes for walking, jogging, or informal occasions.

➤ Pack dark clothes. They don't show spots or dirt and work for most situations.

➤ If you need to be dressed in business attire at your meeting, be sure to wear it on the plane or carry it with you; if your luggage is delayed or lost, you won't be forced to shop.

➤ Sleep smart. Dark circles under your eyes aren't good for business. Carry eye shields and earplugs to counter jet lag or a poor night's sleep in a strange hotel room. Silicone earplugs work best, muting noise, snoring, and annoying chatty airline neighbors. Also, invest in a blow-up pillow to help you sleep soundly on the plane—it will also prevent your hair from being flattened as you sleep, and your neck from getting a crick.

➤ Ask for a hotel room away from the ice machine, elevator, and on the quiet side of the building. It can make a huge difference for your sleep that night and your mood the next day.

➤ Hotel alarm clocks and wake-up services can be unreliable. Pack an inexpensive sports watch with an alarm. Use the stop-watch to time international phone calls as a reminder to keep them short.

➤ Carry C rations. Airlines offer little more than the tiny, salty servings of peanuts or pretzels for short flights. If your flight is delayed or has mechanical problems, you may spend hours on the runway or circling in the air while your stomach is scream-ing. Carry a nutritious and filling power bar and an apple in your briefcase.

➤ Before driving off the lot at the rental car agency, walk around the vehicle to check for dents or other damage. Insist that everything be veri-fied in writing by the rental agent and keep a copy.

➤ If you must leave valuables or luggage in your vehicle, be sure they are locked in the trunk or well hidden.

_____ ⟋⟍⟋ _____

Befriend the bellboys for the most reliable information about the safety of walking from your hotel to a nearby pharmacy, restaurant, or meeting place. They are the best source of information about the neighborhood. Don't hesitate to ask them to walk you there.

◆

Alice Bond, Palm Beach, Florida

➤ Pack more than double the number of business cards you think you will need. Handing someone your card makes a profes-sional statement and immediately establishes your credibility.

➤ Have your business information printed on the reverse side of your cards in the language of the country where you will be doing business.

➤ If you are doing business in Asia, present your business card with both hands. After you accept your colleague's card, carefully and respectfully store it in a good place. Don't just slip it into your back pocket.

➤ The concierge at your international hotel is your best source of local information and help.

➤ How much money do you need? With a bank card or major credit card, you can obtain cash in almost every major city in the world. If you are prone to forgetting your PIN number at home, then write down a coded version in the back of your passport.

Be prepared for the unexpected. Food spills can happen on your clothes anytime and anywhere—in the driver's seat of a car, on the plane, or during a business lunch. Pack an instant stain remover in your purse for quick cleanup. A portable stain removing pen is designed to remove most fresh food and drink stains like coffee, ketchup, barbeque sauce, soy sauce, soda, and tomato juice.

◆

Marybeth Bond

➤ Laptop computers have become a popular item for theft. Stay on the alert, especially when passing through security X-ray machines. A thief watches you place your laptop on the conveyer belt of the X-ray machine, then cuts in line in front of you and sets off the metal detector. While you are delayed, your laptop passes through the machine and a second thief snatches it and quickly disappears. Another technique involves someone spilling coffee or ketchup on you. When you stop and put down your bags to clean it off, be sure your laptop is secured firmly between your legs.

➤ If you will be making several credit card calls from your hotel room, don't hang up between calls, or you will be charged a fee for each call. Most hotel phone systems will allow you to hit the # key for a new dial tone between calls and you will avoid additional charges.

➢ Mix pleasure with your business. When your time is limited, a tour can help you see the best of what the city has to offer and can be a great way to treat a client.

SMART AND SAFE

➢ Business women on the road have safety concerns that men don't.

➢ Look and act confident. Get directions ahead of time and know your destination. If you are unsure of your location, act like you know where you are headed and get directions at a safe-looking gas station, café, or market.

➢ Be aware of your surroundings (people, cars, doorways, stairwells) and have a plan in case you get into a dangerous situation. Be prepared to act quickly, scream for help, kick, and run.

➢ Be proactive, not reactive.

➢ Never volunteer that you are traveling alone. Lie if necessary.

➢ Know where you're going before setting out in a rental car.

➢ Do not reveal a map in your car with a marked route on it.

➢ Write your first initial and last name on your luggage tags to conceal your gender. Or use laminated business cards as luggage tags so that strangers do not know your home address.

➢ Carry your passport, plane ticket, traveler's checks, and cash in a concealed money belt worn under your clothes.

➢ When alone (particularly at night), walk with the crowd and act as if you're part of the pack.

➢ If you will be arriving at night, rental car companies and hotels can arrange for someone to accompany you to and from parking lots.

➤ For peace of mind when traveling alone, choose national hotel chains with interior room entrances, as opposed to motel-style outside entrances. More and more women are also choosing small inns and bed-and-breakfasts where the proprietors are more aware of their activities and will become alarmed if they don't return by a specific time.

➤ When first arriving in your room, hold the door open with your luggage while you check the closets. If you're alone and feel unsafe, ask someone from the front desk to accompany you while you check out your room.

➤ When staying in hotels, always check the window and door locks.

➤ If your hotel room has a sliding door to the outside, make sure it is locked.

➤ Always keep your hotel room door locked. If someone knocks and there's a peephole, look to see who's there. If the person identifies himself as a hotel employee, ask him to come back later, or call the front desk to verify his identity and purpose for coming to your room.

➤ Place the "Do Not Disturb" sign on your door or leave the TV or radio on to discourage anyone from entering your room while you are away.

➤ Keep the curtains in your room closed if your room is located on the first floor or looks out onto a walkway.

➤ If the desk clerk mentions your room number out loud and there are other guests who can overhear, request that you be given a different room and that the clerk not mention the number.

➤ When you're using room service order forms, don't indicate that you're alone or use your first name (which can identify you as a woman).

Before I pack my jewelry, whether it is expensive (or expensive looking), I ask myself if it will fit in or if it will be appropriate in a business setting. In Paris, probably; in Quito, probably not. In some cities, wearing expensive jewelry is an invitation to mugging. Consider the context of where you are going and what you will be doing.

♦

Marybeth Bond

XII
First-Time Travelers

If I had my life to live over again, I'd try to make more mistakes next time.
I would relax. I would limber up. I would be sillier than I have been. I
would take more chances. I would take more trips. I would climb more
mountains, swim more rivers, and watch more sunsets.

—Nadine Stair, "I'd Pick More Daisies"

ALL OVER THE COUNTRY, women of all ages have asked me to give them some words of encouragement to help them step out the door. Some ask, "Do you think I should go?" I tell them "Yes." To boost my self-confidence before I took off on my journey around the world, this is what I did: Every morning as I looked into my mirror, I asked myself, *What's holding you back? What is the worst that could happen? How will you feel about yourself in six months or a year if you don't fulfill your dream? Look at everything you have already accomplished. This is just one more little risk. You know that the first step is the hardest. So quit agonizing over the decision and just go!*

I tell all young people: Travel now while your knees are good and before you settle down. People put off travel for many reasons, but you should do it while you are mobile, active, interested in meeting and learning about people.

♦

Rosemary Gardner,
Oakland, California

TIPS

➤ Before you go, decide honestly what the most important goals are for your trip. Do you want to see lots of sights? Meet as many people as possible? Get to know yourself better? Begin learning a new language? You will be tempted by many choices, but having a clear idea in mind of what you really want from your journey will help you decide what to do and what to skip and you will return home feeling satisfied.

➢ Make a conscious decision about your preferred travel companions. Think through your goals and what you are willing to compromise. Do your homework. Call numerous tour operators, collect and read brochures, read guidebooks, then consider traveling with a like-minded group or alone. One of your most important decisions will be who you travel with. Don't make this decision hastily.

➢ If you choose to travel independently, consider arranging a homestay at the beginning of your trip. It can be as simple as renting a room with a family or arranging an extended stay at a family guesthouse. See the Resources section for a list of organizations that arrange homestays.

➢ Bring one totally impractical thing that makes you feel at home. Travel with a good luck necklace. Throw in a skirt that helps you feel refreshed and energized after wearing the same clothes over and over again.

➢ Make sure your baggage is properly routed at check-in. It is very easy for a tired airline employee to misroute a bag with the wrong destination tag. Learn the particular code for your destination.

➢ If your seatmate on an airplane, bus, or train is driving you nuts with non-

> ——— ⚘ ———
>
> We all share a desire to fulfill our dreams, but few of us act on it. Over and over again women tell me that taking an adventure travel vacation was often the first time they acted on a totally new experience in their lives. For the first time they went somewhere alone, met new people, or learned about another culture. For the first time they experienced an active vacation and physically challenged themselves. They have all come away feeling a newfound and positive sense of self.
>
> ◆
>
> *Susan Eckert, Bozeman, Montana*

stop talk, put on headphones, if you have them, smile, and turn your head away.

➤ In many developing countries you will be hassled by men in airport terminals who offer cheap transportation into town. Don't accept their offers. Seek out a ground transportation desk near the baggage claim area for assistance.

➤ Create cheat sheets for local lingo. It is important to be able to say a few rudimentary words in the local language, such as *please, thank you, beautiful, spicy, not spicy,* and *delicious.* To cheat easily and help you memorize the vocabulary, write basic words on a small sheet of paper or your arm for reference.

➤ When you first arrive in a new city, if you can, take a half-day tour to get oriented.

➤ Before heading out to explore a new city, pick up a business card from your hotel. It's easier than you think to get lost and forget your way back, and a card in your possession will tell taxi drivers or anyone you ask for directions where you want to go. This is particularly important in countries like Thailand, Japan, or China, where you may not be able to read the script and locals may not speak or read English.

➤ Establish routines. Connect to the place you're visiting by going to the same coffee shop every morning and reading the paper. Stroll along the river, waterfront, or town square each evening and you'll start to see familiar faces. It can help you feel a sense of belonging in a new location.

➤ Consider leaving your purse at home and using a small fanny pack, worn around your waist, to carry bills and coins, a hairbrush, lipstick, and other small items. Wear it in front, not behind, which would make it a temptation to pickpockets.

➤ Also carry a small or medium-size backpack for all the things you'll need during the day: journal, camera, water bottle, sweater, guidebook. Select one with a sturdy zipper, several compartments, and padded shoulder straps.

➤ Last-minute purchases in the airport that make a difference: a pack of gum to relieve pressure in your ears, if needed, and for bad breath; postcards of your hometown to share or give away; snacks to stave off midnight hunger while you are adjusting to new mealtimes.

Apply for a passport or check the one you have three to six months before your departure. Numerous countries do not allow entry with a passport considered "soon to expire" (within six months). Handle your passport and visa paperwork long before your departure to avoid paying huge surcharges for last minute services. You may need travel immunizations depending upon where you will be traveling. If they are required for entry into a country, you'll need an International Health Certificate to prove you've gotten all of them, and carry the certificate while traveling. Remember to start your travel immunizations early enough to finish the series of shots before traveling.

Marybeth Bond

XIII
THE STUDENT TRAVELER

Women who travel as I travel are dreamers. Our lives seem to be lives of endless possibility.

Mary Morris, Nothing to Declare

———

TODAY MORE AND MORE TEENS are taking off for semesters abroad, for volunteer programs like Los Amigos or independently to travel through Europe, Asia, or south of the border.

I lived and attended university in Europe (Luxembourg and Paris) for five years in my late teens and early twenties and had marvelous experiences. It was one of the best learning opportunities of my life. To be honest with you, however, my experiences also included sexual verbal harassment, unwanted touching (in crowded buses), inappropriate comments, crude propositions, and a man who exposed himself to me. I learned quickly how to avoid potentially compromising situations and how to dress appropriately.

Recently St. Mary's College in Moraga, California asked me to speak to their university students who are preparing to live or travel abroad. The college felt it was necessary because female students returned from their semesters abroad with negative experiences that could have been avoided. They realized how unprepared so many of their students were regarding the dress code, dating behavior, nightclub etiquette, and safety. Before your departure, it's helpful to understand the stereotypes many foreign men have.

Unfortunately, young North American women are often viewed as naïve, "loose," and craving sex (thanks to American media, television stereotypes, and to revealing fashions). Thus young American women are often targets for sexual come-ons. In some countries women dress more conservatively than we do in North America. Learn about the acceptable women's dress code and "bar behavior" for the country you'll be visiting. Take note of the behavior and dress of young local women. Do they smile at strange men, accept drinks from strangers or show cleavage? What message do you project? Not all men have your best interests at heart. In some cultures a bare belly or tight t-shirt is offensive and may invite nasty advances from the men.

We're also more likely to be the victims of theft, so read on and learn how to protect yourself and your valuables. Pickpockets, scam artists, and smugglers are clever and experienced and usually work in crowded areas so stay alert and hide your valuables.

But don't let fear keep you at home. Make smart choices and use your common sense. Don't be paranoid, but be aware that bad things do happen, and protect yourself. Return home with great pictures, new friends, and positive memories. If you're not a teen, please share these tips with a young friend, niece, neighbor, or daughter.

TIPS

➤ Savor the moment. You've worked hard, and this is your chance to learn about the world in a hands-on way. Fully enjoy yourself and the wonders of the road.

➤ Stay in touch! Calm your concerned mom (or dad, grandmother, friend)—call or email home often.

➤ Are you traveling with friends? Spend part of the day on your own and meet up for dinner. That way, you'll get important time to yourself, have your own stories to tell, and remain appreciative of each others' company.

> ＿ ∖⁄⁄⁄ ＿
>
> Keep your important travel documents, like your passport and electronic ticket itinerary, in the same place, where it's easy to get to them. I stash them in my purse, or the outside pocket of my backpack or carry-on bag.
>
> ◆
>
> *Marybeth Bond*

➤ Don't push your limits where there are no safety nets. For instance, are you an idealist? Prone to political activism? Keep in mind that many countries do not have the democratic liberties of the U.S., and that getting involved in the local politics of a foreign country can be quite dangerous. My advice: Don't. Better to save your hard-core activism for U.S. soil, where you know the rules, the consequences of breaking them, and where help is closer at hand if you need it.

➤ Make smart choices and use your common sense. Don't be paranoid, but be aware that bad things do happen—protect yourself by following your instincts.

➤ Most of the people who offer you food or drink are just being kind. However, the rare exception exists—drugging occasionally happens. Don't leave your drink unattended in bars, and exercise good judgment when accepting food or drink from people.

➤ Be aware of your vulnerabilities as a young woman on the road. For instance, in many countries, it is common for gigolos to prey on young female travelers. Don't be naïve about the intentions of foreign men.

➤ Are you in the mood for love? Make sure it's safe. AIDS is a growing crisis in many developing countries—ALWAYS use a condom.

➤ If you think you are pregnant, get a test. If it is positive, have a second test and then travel to a Western country (like Australia or England) or come home to deal with your options.

➤ How do you know when you've overstayed your welcome at someone's house? Trust your instincts. Servas International, a cultural exchange program, imposes a two-night minimum so you get to know your hosts, and your stay can last as long as it works for both parties. Leave before it is time.

➤ Stay flexible and remember that you can always come home. There's a lot of pressure to continue your travels, but if you're not enjoying yourself, if the trip is not what you expected, you can change your plans en route or come home. Sometimes just giving yourself permission to come home will clarify that you really want to continue traveling. Or you might realize you're just not ready for India yet, and that's okay too. Remember, being gutsy is about being true to yourself.

➤ Most students overseas don't wear baseball hats with logos, "I Love New York" t-shirts, or sweatshirts advertising their university's name. This type of clothing will make you stand out when you want to blend in. Also consider taking one nice outfit for possible nights out.

➤ Leave your expensive or expensive-looking jewelry at home. You don't want a thief to yank it off your neck, wrist, or earlobes.

➤ Crowded buses or trains, the stations, and busy streets are areas where groping or thefts occur. Try to sit or stand next to other women or family groups in restaurants, on trains or buses, and in other public places. It is unlikely that you will be approached or harassed if you're in the company of other people. There is safety in numbers.

——— ᘜᴫᴜ ———

Keep your cash in a secure place, like a money belt, zipped pockets in pants or a vest. Some women sew a pocket into the strap of their bra and stash a few large bills there. Always take your money with you when you leave your seat to go to the toilet in airplanes.

◆

Marybeth Bond

➤ Learn to look gutsy. Even if you feel a little frightened or intimidated, adopt a no nonsense, "don't f.... with me" attitude. Walk with purpose; throw your shoulders back, and chin up and you'll be less of a target for hustlers who prey on disoriented or timid-looking women. If you pretend you're gutsy, you may begin to feel gutsy, too.

➤ Don't leave your street smarts at home, and listen to your inner voice. Trust your instincts. They are well-honed from living in the USA. If you feel something is off, wrong, strange—get out, move on, flee, scream, whatever is appropriate. Do it quickly.

➢ Women should follow simple dress guidelines for travel in Muslim countries. Many Muslim women aren't seen in public and live most of their lives inside, out of view of strange men. (Read *Palace Walk*, part of the Cairo Trilogy by Naguib Mahfouz).

➢ Safe bar behavior differs from country to country. What you can do comfortably in Australia you cannot do safely in Morocco. Ask local female students what's appropriate. In some countries accepting one or more drinks from an unknown man indicates your acceptance to sleep with him. Always go to a bar with a companion and promise you will leave together. Keep an eye on each other and don't go outside the bar for a smoke or a breath of fresh air without your buddy.

> ____ ⁂ ____
>
> In all the Muslim countries in which I have traveled, I stood out as a foreign woman, even when I was modestly dressed. I learned to cover my arms and legs with loose, non-clinging clothing. My young daughters also covered themselves head-to-toe when we traveled in Egypt. I found it helpful to cover my hair in most Islamic countries and to avoid all eye contact with unknown males. All these precautions helped reduce the rude attention from men. When you visit mosques you will be required to cover your hair.
>
> ◆
>
> *Marybeth Bond*

➢ Your student ID (with a photo) will get you discounts in the USA and internationally so don't leave home without it. Many student travelers also purchase the ISIC (International Student Identity Card) for discounts on travel rates, accommodations, museums, cultural venues, entertainment, basic sickness and student travel insurance abroad, and cheap international phone calls. The ISIC card costs approximately $22. (800-223-7986 www.statravel.com).

➤ Carry photocopies of all your important documents just in case they get lost or stolen. And leave copies at home with your family.

➤ Stay in touch! While you're on the road—keep in touch with those you leave behind. Calm your concerned mom or dad. They'll love to hear all about your experiences and to see up-to-date photos of you. You can use any of the free email providers or instant messenger.

> ——— \\\\// ———
>
> What happens if your passport or important documents are stolen or lost? Prepare for this possibility before your departure. Leave copies of your passport, drivers' license, credit and debit cards, and e-ticket itineraries with a family member or someone you can get in touch with easily who will not be traveling. Also scan and email copes to yourself. This way you have two backups.
>
> ◆
>
> *Marybeth Bond*

➤ Pack a small zip lock bag with photos of your friends and family. Include pictures of your home, a birthday party or family get together. When you stay in one place for a few nights, put the photos around your room to create a homey atmosphere filled with friends and loved ones. You'll also meet lots of wonderful people along the way who will want to know more about your life at home and who will enjoy seeing your pictures.

➤ Expect some loneliness or homesickness. It will come and go, like PMS. Don't cut your travels short unless you absolutely have to. Make sure you make the most of your time away. You'll miss friends and family loads, but you do go through phases and as long as you call or email them frequently they'll be okay...and so will you.

➤ Visit the local markets and bazaars for great bargains, colorful displays, and fun people-watching. Jump in and haggle with the vendors for the best price.

➤ To get beneath the surface of a culture, talk to the locals and live like them. Stay in a home, family-run guesthouse or B & B. (See the resource section for homestay organizations). Travel like the locals; walk, bike, take buses or trains. Get up early and go to the market or to a park to join an exercise group. In Hanoi I did Tai Chi every morning with the local senior citizens in a park. We all had a good laugh about my clumsiness.

➤ Take time to talk to local people. You can start with gestures and smiles. It helps if you can learn several words in their language. In my experience, the most important words are: hello, thank you, beautiful, delicious, boy and girl. You can point to a child and say "beautiful" then add with a question in your voice; boy? girl? Or you may touch a woman's handicraft necklace or earrings and say, "beautiful." In Tibet I couldn't quite bring myself to say "delicious" about the yak eyeballs in the soup or the yak butter tea.

XIV
THE SOLO TRAVELER

Traveling alone is not lonely; it's an extremely powerful feeling, very similar to love—it's that kind of strength. It's partly the joy of total alone-ness—not loneliness—of being part of the land, as far as you can see and knowing there's nobody you need share it with.

—Christina Dodwell, Travels with Pegasus

WHEN I STARTED TRAVELING ALONE, at age twenty-nine, it was not by choice. I couldn't find anyone to travel with me. I had two options: stay at home and give up my dream, or go alone. So I swallowed hard, bit my lower lip, and told the world and myself that I could do it. I would do it. I would go alone. I did. And I loved it! I traveled solo for the next two years around the world.

Starting out alone does not mean staying alone. There are many other fascinating people out there traveling by themselves, just like you. At times I would hook up with a kindred spirit and we would travel together for a few days, even for a month. Many of these travel companions are still close friends. My decision to go alone was one of the best choices of my life.

What's so great about it? Solo travelers enjoy the freedom of making all the decisions, experience the world unfiltered by anyone else's perspective, live intensely, meet people more easily and are invited into their lives more readily, avoid difficult travel companions, and get in touch with themselves.

> I have many opportunities to take my husband along on my travels and often do. But when I travel alone, it's an entirely different trip. Instead of being focused on the person with you, you are more observant, more attuned to every sound and detail. And you are much more likely to meet people.
>
> ◆
>
> *Kimberly Brown-Seely,*
> *Seattle, Washington*

Now when I create the opportunity to travel alone, it is a self-indulgent luxury. If you give it a fair chance, you too will discover that solo travel is empowering, intense, and exhilarating.

Divorce or the death of a spouse or partner can leave an avid traveler faced with the same dilemma I had. Do you choose to stay immobilized? Can you find a new travel companion? Or should you go alone? Eventually you'll begin doing day trips alone. In time you may move on to overnights, then longer journeys, until you are surprised and pleased by how confident and happy you are traveling alone.

My marriage dissolved when I was forty-two. That marked the first time I put on a backpack. I knew I had to begin tackling the things I was most afraid of doing alone and travel was number one on my list. I spent five weeks on the road and remember crying a lot. But I also laughed a great deal! I'm fifty-six at this point. I've been traveling solo all this time, except now I wouldn't have it any other way.

♦

Evelyn Hannon, Toronto, Canada

TIPS

➤ You can begin traveling solo at any age. Fortunate are the women who begin traveling alone when they were young. Often they tell me they never experienced any trepidation. For those of you who aren't too sure—try it. Don't let fear stop you. Other travelers on the road and local people will support you and you'll discover how much inner strength you possess.

➤ Consider taking a short trip first to see if you like traveling alone. Find a cute town close by and visit for the weekend. Bring something to read, a journal, and some CDs. Explore your surroundings. Be aware of your solitude and how it feels to be on your own. Then, if you're ready, plan a more adventurous trip. It's O.K. to start small.

➤ Start smart. Even if you want to be unstructured, book at least the first night's accommodation in advance. It will be easier to feel comfortable and get your bearings.

➤ When you travel alone, you accept the responsibility to reach out, be extroverted, and strike up conversations with strangers. You'll find it is much easier to make new friends when you are alone. You are more approachable.

➤ Trust your intuition, no matter what. You will have many great opportunities to explore new places and meet exciting people. One of the best things about travel is being open to these experiences. Just pay attention to your gut when you find yourself in a new situation. It will tell you when to go for it and when to get out. Always listen to your instincts and they will help keep you safe in the midst of your adventures.

➤ Women traveling alone share similar concerns about loneliness, safety, harassment, illness, and accidents. Don't worry. Going alone is not necessarily more dangerous than traveling with a companion—it just requires

_____ ⋇ _____

Everything was magnified by my being alone. In India, exploring a new city on foot, so pleasant in Europe, meant running the gauntlet: hawkers, beggars, insistent merchants came to me from everywhere, invading my personal space. With a companion, such scenes might have been merely local color. A twosome, self-contained, has its own resources. Through conversation and feed-back, it can defuse the impact of the unfamiliar in a way that the solo traveler cannot. Alone and uninitiated, I felt like Snow White assaulted by Disney's animated trees. Every experience was intensely my own, undiluted by the connection to home that a familiar companion supplies. Occasionally I thought, no one on earth knows where I am. That one point held both the exhilaration and the vulnerability of traveling alone.

♦

Jo Broyles Yohay, New York City

extra awareness. You will discover how fine-tuned your survival instincts are. Most countries in the world are not as violent or dangerous as our own. If you need help, ask for it.

➤ Don't travel alone into the backcountry—make sure at least one or two others accompany you. A backcountry injury without someone to help can pose a life-or-death situation.

➤ Buy a popular guidebook. The accommodations and restaurants listed will be full of other independent travelers, so you'll have plenty of opportunities to hook up with a variety of people. You may find yourself exploring the bazaar or eating a meal with your new friends, or you might even travel for a time together. Use your guidebook as an indication of things to see and where to start your journey, then travel farther off the beaten path.

➤ Don't isolate yourself in a hotel or rental car. It's much easier to meet people if you are out and about with locals and other travelers. Use public transportation and stay in hostels, local homes, or bed-and-breakfasts. You will probably meet so many people that you just might yearn for some time alone!

➤ Check out the meeting places for independent travelers. Some guidebooks (such as the Lonely Planet series) will list them. Many cities have well-known meccas for independent travelers, with bulletin boards and unique calendars of local events. These are treasure troves of inex-

_____ ⧼⧽ _____

One of my most memorable encounters in Sri Lanka would not have occurred if I had not been alone and not accepted the kind offer of help from strangers. I was waiting at what I believed to be a bus stop when a man in a battered station wagon filled with cheerful kids stopped and offered me a ride. He informed me that where I was standing was not a bus stop. I accepted his offer because of the presence of his four children. His invitation for a ride to my guesthouse led to a dinner with his wife and a schoolteacher, tours of the island, and a charming friendship.

◆

Marybeth Bond

pensive tours, travel companions or rides wanted, free or almost-free local lectures, and social gatherings, that you can join. A morning jog with the running group "Hash House Harriers" in Singapore or Kathmandu can lead to local friends and social invitations. My hand-written note posted on a message board on a tree in the café courtyard of the Old Stanley Hotel in Nairobi led to a safari with wonderful people and dynamic friendships.

> Every time we set foot on our own as solo travelers, we shave off the edge of oddness and anomaly. We are seen enjoying ourselves, taking care of ourselves. We pave the way for normalcy someday for all those women peeking out from kitchen curtains and behind veils.
>
> ◆
>
> *Joan Medhurst, Alameda, California*

➤ Take advantage of your solo status and be willing to change your plans. One of the greatest things about traveling alone is that you get to do whatever you want to do, all the time. Make an impromptu side trip to the beach. Add an entire country to your anticipated itinerary. Stay in bed all morning on a rainy day. Revel in the joy of not having to compromise.

➤ Treat yourself to small luxuries like high tea at an elegant hotel or a manicure.

➤ When graciously offered, accept spontaneous invitations and hospitality, especially from women or families. Be careful, however, not to overstay your welcome or create a hardship for the family.

➤ How do you handle eating alone in a restaurant? Choose a bistro, café, or lively place. Go prepared with reading and writing materials—postcards, letters, and your journal. Comfortably dining alone is a learned skill. Eventually you'll find yourself enjoying watching people and eavesdropping. And you won't always stay alone after being seated in a restaurant. I have often been invited to join other travelers or vice versa.

➤ Don't be afraid to eavesdrop. It's a great way to identify interesting people with whom you might share something in common. Find a sneaky way to join the conversation.

TIPS FOR OVERCOMING THAT LONELY FEELING

➤ I am often asked, "Do you ever get lonely, and what do you do about it?" I am surprised by how rarely I do get lonely. Remember, just because you are traveling alone doesn't mean you'll be more lonesome than at home.

➤ Fear of being lonely is common and can stop you cold in your tracks. To assuage fears, keep in mind that loneliness is a bit like PMS—predictable, irritating, and temporary.

> I missed meeting a friend at the Lisbon train station and discovered the world of solo travel. Traveling alone, I think the smells are sharper, the sounds more distinct, the flavors more powerful, and the people much friendlier.
>
> ◆
>
> *Kari Bodnarchuk,*
> *Bellingham, Washington*

➤ Different moments in your trip will require different approaches to coping with loneliness. Sometimes it's important not to sink into your loneliness. To counter loneliness, stay active. Take a walk in a park, eat in lively, crowded restaurants, initiate conversations with strangers, and shop for gifts for your friends and family. Other times giving in to your mood is the best possible medicine. At times like this, I become reclusive, reading, listening to music, writing in my journal or to friends and family.

➤ When you're feeling low, I don't recommend calling home. It can make you feel worse. But writing postcards or sending an e-mail from a cybercafé is uplifting.

➤ Take care of yourself. When I start to feel lonely, it's often because I haven't eaten or slept enough or I've had too much caffeine. If I stay well fed, fit, and rested, then depression, loneliness, and illness are usually avoided.

➤ Treat yourself. I will pamper myself with a hot bubble bath, buy a new book and dig into it, or have a massage or manicure. In India and Thailand I bought garlands of gardenias and richly fragrant flowers for my room. In Chicago I got dressed up and went to a posh hotel for a drink and hours of people watching.

➤ Write in a journal. When you find yourself missing your best friend at home, write down everything you want to tell her in your journal. Don't just put down what you saw that day—include how you're feeling about yourself and your trip. If you want to go home, write about it! Periodically read back over your journal and see how your journey is unfolding. Take yourself out to dinner when you realize how fabulous you are!

> ⎯⎯ ⧯ ⎯⎯
>
> Recognize the difference between solitude and loneliness. I made the choice to be alone and I like my own company. Now I cherish my time alone and accept the lonely moments. They never last long. They come and go, just like at home.
>
> ◆
>
> *Marybeth Bond*

⎯⎯ ⧯ ⎯⎯

Alone we can afford to be wholly whatever we are and to feel whatever we feel absolutely.

◆

May Sarton, Poet

XV
WOMEN TRAVELING TOGETHER

One of the great things about travel is you find out how many good,
kind people there are.

—*Edith Wharton*

AT MY SPEAKING ENGAGEMENTS the conversation inevitably turns toward women traveling together. For many women, traveling with other women takes the fear out of seeing the world. Women always ask how they can meet other women travel companions. They are single, divorced, or widowed; their husbands aren't interested in travel; or their friends won't travel without their husbands. Now more than ever women are interested in finding other women to travel with.

I encourage women to meet other women for the sole purpose of travel. Find someone who shares your passion for wandering the globe or for weekend getaways. Or meet someone local who has similar interests—for example, photography—and go on a photography travel expedition together. There are many travel companies that specialize in planning trips specifically for women (see the Resources section for more information). These trips are a lot of fun and chances are you will meet others that you might want to travel with in the future.

A different kind of bonding unfolds on an all-women trip. Last spring I traveled for twelve days in France with seven women I didn't know. I laughed more in those twelve days than I had in the last twelve months. Traveling with women is a different and wonderful kind of fun. So if you're married and your husband doesn't like to travel, leave him at home. He'll be there when you get back.

♦

Marybeth Bond

New friendships are formed on the road, and life-long relationships deepened. A getaway with your girlfriends can be a wonderful thing, one that will remind you why you've been friends for so long. It gives you a chance to spend quality time together and gives you an increased comfort level while traveling. When you travel with other women, be open to self-discovery and self-revelation. Get to know the women you are traveling with and share your life experiences with them. This part of the journey holds wonderful possibilities. Enjoy your time bonding with the other women on the trip, and be open to meeting even more women in the destinations to which you are traveling.

TIPS

➤ Before you and your travel companions leave, acknowledge that problems may arise and discuss how you will deal with them. Be honest about your "hot buttons" (people being bossy, chronic lateness) and agree to be sensitive to each other's particular needs. Be open when something is bothering you and address it immediately. Talk issues through and don't let them fester. Then let them go and enjoy your trip.

➤ When traveling with others, it's always good to set boundaries before you go. If you know that you need personal quiet time each day, then be sure to articulate this to your travel partner. That way she won't take it personally and will know that you simply need your space. See "Roommate Rules" below for more information.

➤ Don't assume that you can borrow your travel partner's make-up, brush, shampoo, conditioner, toothpaste, or clothes. Just because you are traveling together, that doesn't mean her items are up for grab. Be respectful and ask permission if you would like to borrow something.

➤ To make more room in your luggage, discuss items that you might be able to share with your traveling companion. She can bring the hair dryer, and you'll pack the binoculars.

➢ Take off on your own for a few days. You might be interested in exploring Venice, while she would rather stay in Florence. Don't limit your itinerary. Travel solo and arrange to reconvene at a specific time and place.

➢ Seek out women to talk to while you travel—on trains, in restaurants or cafés, or while shopping. You will learn a lot from local women that will enhance your travels. They are usually as pleased to meet you as you are to meet them.

➢ If you want to meet women in larger cities, make a quick check of local directories under the headings "female," "woman," or "travel." This can produce wonders. You'll probably find listings for craft collectives, women's bookstores, and women's organizations.

➢ If you are a lesbian traveling with your significant other and you are worried about the treatment you will receive if the nature of your relationship is known, then do not reveal the truth. In some cultures, it may be better to hide your relationship than take the risk of being harassed, mistreated, or physically harmed.

ROOMMATE RULES

➢ When you find out who your roommate will be, call her and introduce yourself. This is a good time to tell her a bit about yourself and delicately and honestly to approach the topic of snoring. Ask her, "Do you snore?" Better to find out before the trip and take along earplugs, or find another roommate, than to find out the first sleepless night.

➢ On the first day establish ground rules, including showering times, choosing beds, storage space, and dividing the bathroom counter space. That way there is no misunderstanding.

➢ Describe your preferred "morning mood." I am silent and greatly appreciate quiet or soft conversations; I like to exercise in the morning, so when you wake up I may be gone. This way she won't worry if she wakes up and you aren't there.

➤ Promise to give one another some time alone in the room every day. This should be a minimum of thirty minutes. Set up an agreeable schedule ahead of time, and when it is your turn to give your roommate her time, go for a walk, read, or write postcards in the lobby or a local café.

➤ Just because you are roommates, you don't have to spend all of your time together. Communicate clearly that you came on the trip to meet a lot of new people.

When Linda, Priscilla, and I were well into our second girl trip a few years ago, my two friends found a rack of colorful stretch bracelets in a hip store on Wisconsin's Washington Island. The bracelets were silver, set with little sparkles of green, blue, pink, and gold. Each of us chose one and gleefully put it on as a trip souvenir and emblem of our special sisterhood. Since then, we've found orange, yellow, green, and blue glass bead bracelets at an Indian Pow Wow in Tama, Iowa, and lush Venetian glass bracelets in Stockbridge, Massachusetts. We'll keep gathering bracelets as long as we can. We feel a slight regret that we didn't catch this inspiration on our first trip—hiking the Long Trail in Vermont to celebrate our sixtieth birthdays.

◆

Linda Borcover, Evanston, Illinois

XVI
THE 60+ TRAVELER

Age is not determined by the passing of years, but by our reactions to new ideas—our resistance to change. People grow old through their encasement in the past—not in their hopes for the future. Years may wrinkle the skin; but to give up faith, courage, ambition, enthusiasm for the future, and the spark of continuing growth wrinkles the soul!

—*Pacific Crest Outward Bound School*, Book of Readings

IN MY GRANDMOTHER'S DAY, the only acceptable travel for a middle-aged or older woman was to visit Aunt Pearl in a nearby town. Normal women in their sixties and seventies didn't hike in New Zealand, bike in New England, join a study tour to Spain, or travel alone! Bus tours and cruise ships were the predominant form of "mature" travel. Society has changed. Today, as 60+ Americans stay more active and mature women become more gutsy, your imagination is the limit.

An experienced septuagenarian traveler, Betty Ann Webster, once told me, "I have traveled with my husband and children, with friends of many countries, with a forty-year-old son, and enjoyed all those trips. I've often found white hair and advanced age an advantage. For instance, I

Age is no barrier to your dreams and goals.

♦

Helen Thayer,
author of Polar Dream

am never hassled by men as younger women traveling by themselves sometimes are. On the contrary, I'm often helped, whether I need it or not. Young Asians call me 'Aunty.' I have never encountered violence, either physical or verbal. Traveling, especially alone, involves risk, trust, judgment, and probably luck. But doesn't life itself, wherever you are?"

Grandparents are also spending valuable time with their grandchildren traveling. Travel presents an invaluable opportunity to get to know your grandchildren in unique contexts. Indeed, more and more intergenerational families are taking to the road, the skies, the seas, and the rails...and loving it. Everyone is enriched by cross-generational bonding, grandparent mentoring, and different generations learning and exploring together.

No matter how old you are, it's never too late to travel.

TIPS

➢ The world's your oyster! If you're retired, you can travel any season and, if you want, avoid other tourists. Take advantage of your flexibility.

➢ If you plan to travel with a group, at the time you're doing your research be sure to ask about "single supplements." Several soft adventure travel companies will not charge you an extra fee if they cannot find you a roommate. (See Resources section for names, addresses, and phone numbers of tour operators.)

➢ Look for special-interest tours and groups or organize a journey around a special passion.

➢ Ask the tour company for a list of passengers who have gone on the tour you wish to take. Call several of them and ask them what they thought of the trip.

➢ Youth hostels are not just for youth. They offer safe, clean, friendly lodging all over the world.

> _____ ◌◍ _____
>
> At age sixty, I flew with a friend to Jasper, Alberta, and we rode our bikes to Denver—1,800 miles. We crossed the Continental Divide six times. Before we left, everyone told us not to go, that it wouldn't be safe for two women alone. In five weeks no harm came to us. One of the important things I learned was how material things can become an encumbrance and how little you need to get along. I recommend to anyone, any age, if you have a dream, you mustn't put it off five years. Everybody, please, follow your dreams.
>
> ◆
>
> _Mary Mulligan, Denver, Colorado_

➢ Traveling by recreational vehicle is increasingly popular with many elder adventurers. Consider renting an RV to try it out. You can become a member of an RV association and travel with other RVers or learn RV maintenance.

➢ A medical emergency abroad can be quite frightening. Take out trip insurance that offers emergency evacuation.

➢ Carry a list of phone numbers and addresses for U.S. embassies and consulates in the region in which you're traveling. You can contact them for emergency services. They can also help you find a reputable local doctor, dentist, or hospital.

➢ As a 60+ traveler, the deals await you! Travel presents a great opportunity to flaunt your age and save your money. Just remember to ask if there's a deal.

On recent trips to Turkey and British Columbia, I wore a fanny pack instead of carrying a purse. The relief I felt in never worrying "Where is my purse?" was inestimable.

◆

Ruth Bond, Akron, Ohio

As a senior citizen, you should know that Medicare does not cover medical expenses overseas. When you travel, be sure to get a policy that will cover you while you are abroad.

◆

Olga Murray, Sausalito, California

ON THE ROAD WITH THE GRANDKIDS

➢ Share stories of the "olden days." Relate historic events—the first moon landing, Woodstock, and so forth—to enhance your grandchildren's studies.

➢ Tell your grandchildren stories about their mom and dad when they were young—this can create a strong link between past and present. Try the following theme: "Let me tell you a story about when your (mother or father) was bad." Children take special delight in hearing about the behavior of their parents, especially the naughty stuff.

➤ Take a lot of pictures and videos.

➤ Set rules you are comfortable with, even if they are different from their parents'.

➤ You might need more downtime than those feisty squirts—take the grandkids to a park so they can meet children their own age.

———— ☼ ————

A delightful side effect of developing a shock of white hair is that other travelers often feel a need to help an older woman. Never mind that I'm on my way to shoot the rapids of a wild New Zealand river or explore an ancient shipwreck with a scuba partner. When I patiently listen to a teenager giving directions to a place from which I've just come, it creates a bond that invites further interaction. I've made friendships, uncovered new places, sampled exotic fare, just because for a moment I traded my need to assert self-assurance for the exhilaration of discovery.

◆

Judy Wade, Phoenix, Arizona

———— ☼ ————

Many grandparents choose to take their grandchildren on organized tours or cruises where there will be other kids, organized children's activities, and some downtime for the adults. See the Resource and Reference section for recommended tour operators, cruises, and dude ranches for "Family Travel."

◆

Marybeth Bond

XVII
MOTHER-DAUGHTER TRAVEL

From grandma and her maternal line, I inherited the urge to keep moving.
For the women in my family, getting away from the ordinary provides
impetus to wander. Travel exemplifies freedom.

Vera Marie Badertscher, "Traveling Woman," A Mother's World

MORE AND MORE WOMEN are taking to the road in mother-daughter pairs. And with good reason. If you want to know about the inner life of your mother or daughters, you need almost endless opportunities to talk. The journey you take will be to the center of yourself and your relationship. The memories you will cherish for a lifetime.

I was twenty-six when my mother and I took our first trip together—just the two of us. She left my dad in Ohio and came to visit me. We spent the weekend exploring gold-mining towns in the foothills of the Sierra Nevada mountains. We talked and laughed almost every waking moment. Quite by accident, we came upon a river-rafting group preparing to ride the rapids down the Stanislaus River. Without a moment's hesitation, my mother said, "I've always wanted to do this. Let's see if we can join them!" We spent the afternoon shooting the rapids. And I spent months reflecting upon how little I knew about my responsible, schoolteacher mother.

Laura and I have a wonderful time traveling together, but at times it is a challenge for me to travel "college style." Laura, of course, does not have any trouble adjusting to the luxury hotels to which I've become accustomed. The pleasure of traveling with my daughter is how her openness to new adventures off the beaten path affects me.

♦

Lenore Thornton, New York City

Few things are more rewarding, so don't hesitate to do it.

TIPS

➤ Offer your mother the priceless gift of your time. Treat her to a night away—just the two of you. Plan an activity that will be very special for both of you: an elegant dinner, a play, a nice hotel, or a river-rafting trip.

➤ If your short excursions together are successful, consider traveling together for longer periods, perhaps even booking an organized tour to someplace you both have always wanted to go.

➤ Begin an annual tradition of taking your mother or daughter, or both, on an overnight adventure. Try camping if you enjoy the outdoors or stay at a resort close to home. You might choose a date near Mother's Day or her birthday.

➤ Be honest up front about how to avoid stepping on one another's toes. If your mom hates the way you drive, hand over the keys. If you're miserable unless you have a window seat, let her know before she books the tickets. Talking openly about your trip in advance will allow you to focus on enjoying your time together.

—— ⚬⚬⚬ ——

Wherever my sister, mom, and I go, we look for thrift shops. We check in the phone book for "thrift stores." My sister will give each of us $20 and we'll go in and shop for each other, and when we go home we wrap up our treasures and present them to each other. Then we hoot and laugh and exchange or trade the items. We have found all sorts of goodies: brand new Stewart Wiseman black alligator shoes for $3.50 or a Coach Bag for $4, a Dunny Burke Purse for $19 and an Armani jacket sample for $15. The best thrift shops we've found are on Main Street, Ventura, California, however, we found a unique store in Sedona with Southwestern clothes. We're looking forward to our next trip to San Francisco to investigate a store that caught our attention: "Out of the Closet."

◆

Kathy Musser, Akron, Ohio

➤ Give one another space. Just because you're on a trip together doesn't mean that you have to spend every moment in shared company. Create time in the day for each of you to do your own thing. At times you may consider getting separate rooms so you can have the evening to quietly reflect and reenergize.

➤ Bring along books and music that you can enjoy together. If you're on a longer trip, you and your mother can each bring a few books and then trade. Discuss your opinions of your shared readings during long rides and over meals.

➤ If your mother is a widow and you are single, and you usually spend the holidays together, consider exploring a new corner of the world instead of staying home. A friend of mine, a widow in her seventies, and her daughter, in her thirties, spend every Christmas holiday making memories—from tramping around Anasazi ruins in the Southwest to cruising in the Indonesian islands.

➤ If you can work it out, take your daughter on a short business trip. You can show her what your professional life is like away from home and how you use caution to navigate safely in an unfamiliar city. You can share the places you enjoy, such as museums, parks, cafés, and restaurants.

> For me, the best thing about traveling with my mama is sharing a bed and cuddling.
>
> ◆
>
> *Annalyse Sheppard,*
> *Marin, California*

➤ One of the most rewarding aspects of taking a mother-daughter trip is the way we travel. We dawdle along the road; we pause to stop and stare; we relax over a pot of tea, watching people, being quiet or talking about the idiosyncrasies of life. Be sure to allow for unstructured time in your itinerary.

➤ If you are traveling with your mother, ask her about her youth, her teenage years, her romances. Share some of your more private memories with her.

➤ Take your mom on the trip she fantasizes about. If she's always wanted to see her grandmother's birthplace in Mexico, surprise her with a plane ticket and your companionship.

➤ I try to take each of my daughters individually on a mother-daughter outing every year. I love these trips. They give me the opportunity to focus on one child at a time and appreciate how she is growing and our relationship is changing. There is no sibling rivalry and she

The best thing about my travels with my mother is that I am always expecting to show her my world and my experiences, living in another country (Thailand), but instead we end up creating new experiences and discovering a world of our own.

♦

Laura Thornton, Singapore

has all of my attention. The sibling left at home, of course, is being spoiled rotten by her dad, who is having special father-daughter time with her. It is healthy for everyone in the family. Don't wait until they're grown.

Mama's passport photo says it all. The impish grin is brighter than the white curls, the wrinkle of smile deeper than the wrinkles of age. She's happy. She's going somewhere. With me. The mug shot proves I shouldn't have waited so long to invite her. We'd talked about a big trip we'd take "sometime," but I married and got even busier at home and work, and summers and years passed with no adventure together. Then Daddy died. Out of those sad days of winter came a sense of urgency. Time and life were galloping past, and I needed to catch up.

♦

Mary Ellen Botter, Prosper, Texas

XVIII
TRAVEL WITH CHILDREN

It is a wise parent who gives her children roots and wings.
—*Chinese Proverb*

BEFORE WE HAD KIDS, my husband and I were sure our style of travel wouldn't change; we would just haul our children with us—everywhere. But along with the sleepless nights, diapers, bibs, blankets, and colic came a foreboding premonition that I would never travel again in any way. Although my children haven't exactly stopped me, they have slowed me down (sometimes for the better). I have learned when to take them along and when to go alone.

I am a strong advocate of numerous family vacations each year. Unfortunately, our trips are usually short. But I feel almost any getaway is worth the hassle.

Let me clarify what I mean by *family*. I don't just mean the "Ozzie and Harriet" nuclear family of mom, dad, and 2.4 children. Today's family may be any combination of children with a single parent, significant others, friends, or grandparents.

> To protect your children, don't travel with hats, bags, or backpacks that display their names. A stranger could call your child by name, gain his/her confidence more easily, and convince your child you sent the stranger to get them.
>
> ◆
>
> *Marybeth Bond*

Some of the gutsiest women I know and admire are single moms who travel with their children all the time, almost everywhere. At a book signing in Fairlawn, Ohio, a single mom told me her story of driving to Alaska with her three-year-old daughter and camping for two months. I was humbled by her courage. She was still amazed and empowered by her adventure. Such stories are not unusual. I applaud every mom who has taken her children camping or traveling on her own.

Traveling with children is very different from traveling by yourself, with your spouse, or with a friend. Although you may, as I did, have great trepidation about traveling with your children, you will soon learn that the rewards and memories are worth every inconvenience. My children have opened up new worlds for me. They have given me a different and refreshing perspective on everything we do and see. Together we make more friends and feed off each other's energy and adventurous spirits.

TIPS

> Everyone should be involved—from planning the trip and packing to making decisions on the road. As soon as you know where you are going, involve your children: check out books and magazines from your library, mark up a map, discuss what distance you will travel, how long it will take to get there, and what they will do during this time. Let the kids take part in the selection of the toys, games, books, and art materials you take along.

> Children learn responsibility when they compose their own packing lists and pack their own bags. It builds confidence and decision-making skills. Show them your lists and discuss how you are packing and making plans in advance. They can make sure that their favorite clothes are clean the day before departure. It is a good idea to confirm that they have the essentials.

> Plan age-appropriate activities. Each day should include something of interest for everyone. Take into consideration your youngest child's interests and abilities and then work your way through the interests of each family member, including yourself.

> Rest and relaxation should be high on your list of activities.

_____ ⋰⋱ _____

Traveling is your children's best teacher. When they observe how other people live in other places, they not only learn about the wider world but about their world, too. Just don't expect them to express their thanks for the trips you've taken together. Appreciation will only come later in life.

◆

Claire Walter, Boulder, Colorado

Plan quiet time or naps. Picnics are a great way to slow down your pace. Find a park where they can run around and meet other kids while you put your feet up and read some of your book.

➤ Keep it simple. Underplan your days and move at a leisurely pace so you don't feel rushed. Traveling with children, you won't be able to see or do as much as you would without them. They need extra time to get dressed, go to the bathroom, have snacks, and work off extra energy.

Traveling with children requires not only love but extra patience and ingenuity, especially ingenuity, to keep them occupied and to replace the comforting routines of home.

♦

Ruth Bond, Akron, Ohio

➤ You can simplify your life if you locate and use the restrooms as soon as you arrive at an attraction or museum.

➤ Snacks and filling food are essential. If you feed them, they will be happy. At all times carry drinks and stick-to-your-ribs snacks like apples, bagels, or low-fat granola bars.

➤ It is helpful to set expectations for a vacation prior to departure. Discuss how things will be different where you are going. Prepare your kids for new kinds of food, entertainment, toilets, languages, long travel days, and periods of "down time." Children are more agreeable if they know what to expect.

Getting through the security check at the airport with a small child, diaper bag, stroller, or car seat is not easy. Avoid wearing jeans with metal studs or a belt with a metal buckle to avoid further delays or hassles.

♦

Marybeth Bond

➤ On long trips, children get by with very few clothes or

toys and they learn how little they really need to be happy. Encourage them to pack lightly.

➤ When traveling, children quickly learn that their favorite foods and entertainment are not available everywhere, and that some of their favorite foods may indeed be considered disgusting by others—and vice versa. Most kids will try new foods and abandon picky eating habits. They will discover new and simple ways to entertain themselves.

➤ If you are traveling long distances by car with small children, and you want to arrive at your destination with time to spare, rise at 4:30 or 5:00 A.M. and pack your vehicle before everyone else awakes. Pack swimsuits and pajamas in separate bags so they are easily accessible. This way you will not have to break down all your bags to get at one item.

➤ Learn some elements of the language as a family before you travel to a foreign country. Your children will not only benefit from beginning to learn a new language, they will get to use it practically and make friends more easily, even if they know only a few key phrases and words.

➤ If an extended trip is not possible, take your child to a local ethnic market or check out a culture-appropriate video from the library.

➤ History "sticks" when children actually see where it took place. Being in a noteworthy place makes a far stronger impression than most books can. Background material will enhance the experience, however, so check out relevant books from the library before you go.

➤ Stop at tourist information booths or offices. Your children can pick up brochures and create scrapbooks from them. You may also learn about a festival or museum—or cave—you were unaware of (and may discover a family member has an interest you never suspected).

➤ Travel teaches kids to take pleasure from exploring the natural world—watching a tide pool, collecting pinecones to make forest dolls, rolling down grassy hillsides, seeing an eagle hunt. Try to spend unstructured time outdoors.

➤ Trips are a great way to make geography come alive. Show your children the intended route on the map and explain how long it will take to go from point A to point B. Use city and state maps for shorter excursions. Get a felt-tip pen and draw your route; it will be a wonderful souvenir and memory prompt later, even if it is in tatters.

➤ Kids learn about other cultures by exposure to them: attending a rodeo in Wyoming, observing a tribal powwow in New Mexico, staying in a home in Ireland, visiting a pottery workshop in Mexico, meandering through a market in any developing country, or buying hot, fresh tortillas at a *tortilleria* in Baja.

In our family, we have a slogan: "If it is free, we go and see; if you have to pay, we stay away." State parks, national forest campgrounds, and motels in small towns are bargains.

◆

Doris Scharfenberg,
Farmington Hills, Michigan

➤ For really picky eaters, consider offering the child a coin in the local currency for every new food they try. Is this a bribe? Yes!

➤ Kids need lots of physical activity. Carry action toys—such as a frisbee, inflatable beach ball, or tennis ball—with you at all times for an impromptu sports game.

➤ Buy postcards in the airport or in gift shops and bring stationery. Travel time is great for writing to pen pals, friends, or grandparents.

➤ Travel teaches children how to be flexible as the family encounters delays, cancellations, reservation mix-ups, closed attractions, full restaurants, rude people. They will learn to remain calm and enjoy the adventure if *you* do.

➤ Memories are made from such brief moments. A trip of only a few short days or weeks in reality will last a lifetime. Children will never forget learning how to make a campfire, bathing under a waterfall, eating mangoes on the beach under a full moon, walking across an airport tarmac, or mimicking unforgettable characters on the road.

When you arrive at a museum, head for the gift ship. Have your children look through the postcards depicting artwork in the museum's collection and pick out five of their favorites, then have them search for them on your tour of the museum. This makes the visit much more enjoyable.

◆

Carole Terwilliger Meyers,
Oakland, California

➤ Traveling together will change your family. You will discover each other as individuals and appreciate each other's unique characteristics. So keep a record of the trip and the changes you observe in each other. Describe funny situations, conversations, and memorable comments that each person makes in your travel journal.

Traveling with my daughters to an art museum is different than when I was a child. I allow my girls to speak out and explore. If you stop and see things through their eyes, as opposed to making them see the world through adult eyes, you will learn something not only about the world, but about each other. This is a travel experience you will bring home and keep for life.

◆

Christine Loomis, Boulder, Colorado

SAFETY FIRST

➤ In a car, always buckle up your children, no matter how much they protest. A person is four times more likely to be killed and thirteen times more likely to be injured when thrown from a car.

➤ Keep your baby in the car safety seat. Stop if you have to feed or comfort your baby. A 10-pound infant in a three mile per hour crash would be ripped from your arms with a force of 200 pounds.

➤ Safety belts are made for one person. Children should not share them.

➤ Don't use pillows or cushions to boost your child.

➤ Stop for frequent rests, exercising, and toilet breaks.

➤ Children should carry their own identification inside their packs, in purses, or sewn into their clothing.

➤ Kids and ticks go together like peanut butter and jelly. Although most ticks are harmless, Lyme disease, caused by the bite of a rare and tiny tick, is a serious concern for every parent. Be prepared when hiking in unfamiliar areas. Prevention is not always easy. It is recommended that you and your kids wear long sleeves and long pants in the woods and grassy areas. Take a shower after being outside and check yourself and your child carefully.

➤ If you do find a tick, remove it gently but firmly with tweezers. Take your time. If you pull too hard or twist, you may leave the head embedded in the body. Wipe the skin with antiseptic. Keep the tick. Put it in a jar to show medical authorities later if necessary. Watch for any skin reaction or any unusual symptoms and contact a physician immediately if they occur.

➤ On family vacations it seems that everyone gets a large dose of sunshine, but sunburn for a child is serious. Pack lots of sunscreen (SPF fifteen or greater); use it thirty minutes before going into the sun and reapply every two hours, even if the product is touted as waterproof. Cloudy days are just as dangerous as sunny days.

➤ Always pack a broad-brimmed hat or bonnet to protect your child's face, ears, and scalp. Keep babies out of the sun entirely.

➤ Bees love sweets, watermelon, and burgers. So do kids. What do you do when the two meet? Remove the stinger with a horizontal scraping motion, using your fingernail or something flat like a driver's license. Don't squeeze or pull the stinger or you'll release more venom. Clean the site with soap and water and apply ice compresses. Make a paste of unseasoned meat tenderizer or baking soda (if you happen to have some with you) and water and apply to the area. This will neutralize the remaining venom.

➤ When traveling with kids your first-aid kit should include tweezers (with pointed tips), bandages, gauze, fancy Band-aids, antibacterial soap, adhesive tape, first aid/antibacterial cream or ointment, child- and adult-strength ibuprofen or aspirin, syrup of ipecac (for poison), thermometer, age-appropriate motion sickness medication, sunscreen, and antihistamine for allergic reactions. A bottle of unseasoned meat tenderizer is handy for bee or wasp stings. Zip-lock bags make quick ice packs with a hand towel for a cover.

➤ When you arrive at theme parks, museums, and other crowded tourist attractions, select a central meeting place just in case you get separated from your kids. Counsel them on how to identify and approach an employee to ask for help if they think they are lost. If they need to locate you in a crowd, advise them to call you by your first names. There will be lots of other mommies and daddies.

➤ Have your children memorize the name of your hotel. Give them a hotel business card to keep in their pocket.

➤ Encourage your kids to wear bright-colored tops so they are more visible in a crowd.

XIX
VOLUNTEER TRAVEL

Never doubt that a small group of thoughtful, committed citizens can
change the world. Indeed, it is the only thing that ever has.

—Margaret Mead

SOMETIMES UNSTRUCTURED, FREE-WHEELING TRAVEL is as
good as it gets—a delicious break from the regimens of our busy, over-
planned lives. Other times nothing surpasses the rewards of planting
yourself in one place and digging in. For travel with a meaningful
twist, consider volunteering or joining theme-oriented journeys.

If you're craving a deeper connection to the places you're visiting, ready to throw yourself into a project, and excited to meet and
work with people from all over the world, I highly recommend volunteering during your travels.
Volunteering on the road can require as minimal a commitment
as a day or as extensive a commitment as a couple of years. It
all depends on what you want to
do and the flexibility of your
plans. Yet, regardless of the
length or nature of your volunteer stint, it will likely be one of
the most rewarding parts of your
trip. Volunteering feeds the soul.
It immerses you more deeply
than you could imagine and will
leave its imprint long after the
project ends.

Many international organizations offer an array of volunteer
and work-abroad options as far-ranging as an archaeological dig in

> Teaching in Japan gave me a
> depth of knowledge and insight
> into the culture that I would not
> otherwise have gained, even
> through years of study. While
> not always easy, nothing else I've
> done has been nearly as worth-
> while or rewarding. I learned at
> least as much as I taught, and I
> left with some of the most vivid
> memories and deepest friend-
> ships of my life.
>
> ◆
>
> *Tara Weaver,*
> *San Francisco, California*

Israel, trail maintenance in Yellowstone National Park, school-building in Nicaragua, caring for the dying at Mother Teresa's hospice in Calcutta, museum restoration in England, and teaching English in Tunisia. Volunteer possibilities are innumerable—what matters is finding the right match for you.

TIPS

➢ Determine your interests, needs, and reasons for volunteering. The clearer you are about what you want, the more likely you'll choose your project well, and the less likely you'll feel disappointed or frustrated by your experience.

➢ Take into account your abilities and limitations—emotional, physical, intellectual, and financial. For instance, do you have a bad back? If so, a project involving hard manual labor and lots of bending—such as building a house—might not be for you. Likewise, if you're highly skilled at working with people, consider putting that ability to use in your volunteer work.

➢ Research the organizations you come across and try to avoid committing to the first opportunity that pops up. You want to know as much as possible about the organization with which you work and feel confident about what you're getting yourself into.

> When you travel, connecting with the local people draws you out of yourself and into their world. And when you go back home, your own world is wider and richer for it.
>
> ♦
>
> *Claire Martin,*
> *Santa Monica, California*

➢ Talk to alumni of whatever organization/project you're considering. Some of the most honest and accurate evaluations of a program come from those who have gone before you, who have already invested their time, energy, and money. Their experience and wisdom is often invaluable.

➤ Find out how long the organization has been around. Is its work well respected? Will you feel good about having an affiliation with this organization?

➤ How much money are you willing or able to spend? The financial costs of volunteer projects vary considerably. Some volunteer opportunities are free, whereas others cost more than a package tour. Don't forget to take into account the cost of getting to the work location.

➤ How do you feel about groups? Most volunteer projects involve working closely with a group of strangers. (Of course they won't be strangers for long!) Working together can be one of the most rewarding ways to get to know people, including those from different countries and backgrounds, but also one of the most challenging. As with all travel, it helps to be flexible, open, and up for the adventure.

➤ Find out how much time you'll have to yourself. Will you have days off? An hour of solitary time each day? Or will most of your time be determined by the structure of the program? How many hours per day are you expected to work? Is there any flexibility?

➤ Are you traveling with your family? Ask if kids can participate. If not, is there something else for them to do in the area?

➤ Don't expect things to operate exactly as they do back home. While the differences may be charming to the short-term visitor or tourist,

When you volunteer in a foreign country you are welcomed into the homes and hearts of local people. You begin a journey to the depths of your soul.

◆

Marybeth Bond

those volunteering or working abroad for long stints may get frustrated when systems do not function in familiar ways. Be prepared and, when it happens, relax. This is an opportunity to learn how things work locally and how to approach the situation next time around.

➤ Realize that it may not be possible to accomplish as much as you initially planned—not that you shouldn't try! Language, cultural differences, tradition, and pace of life may prove challenging obstacles to your original objectives. If this happens, don't despair. Reevaluate your goals and focus on what is achievable, given the specifics of the situation. There is no failure in altering your plans once you've learned what is truly possible and worth pursuing.

> ____ ⚓ ____
>
> I volunteered to work on a small organic farm in remote Far North Queensland, Australia. The work was hard, it poured every day, and I got attacked by biting ants. Still, I loved being outdoors all the time, doing valuable work, and getting way off the tourist track.
>
> ◆
>
> *Michelle Snider,*
> *Oakland, California*

➤ While travelers often exist in a constant state of discovery, when you settle into a place for longer stretches it is possible to slip into a daily pattern. Don't lose sight of the incredible opportunity you have to explore your host culture. Make a list of things you want to accomplish in your time overseas, whether it's studying traditional arts or languages, visiting specific places, or experiencing special events or festivals. By organizing your time and setting goals, you can make sure your time is well spent—it will be over before you know it!

➤ Check out the International Volunteer Programs Association (IVPA) at *www.volunteerinternational.org*. IVPA is an alliance of nonprofit organizations offering a great range of international volunteer and internship opportunities. For other reputable organizations doing good work around the world, turn to the Resources section.

THEME-ORIENTED TRAVEL

➤ Theme-oriented travel presents another good way to deepen and focus your experiences on the road. It allows you to connect travel to your passions or nurture a fledgling interest.

➤ Do you love to cook? Are you fascinated by Thailand? Why not attend a cooking school in Bangkok? Is the Maine coast your favorite place to vacation, and you've just picked up photography? The seaside village of Rockport hosts one of the most extensive photography programs in the country. Are you dying to learn Spanish, as well as tromp around for a few months with a backpack? Why not enroll in a language-immersion school in Quito, Ecuador? You'll be surprised by how quickly you learn the language in such an intensive context, and then you can explore South America with new communication skills.

➤ Consider what type of vacation you want when selecting your tour, trek, language program, holistic center, or painting workshop. Do you want something intensive or relaxed? Something solitary or with a group? Would you rather spend a weekend away or a month? As always, the clearer you are about your wants and needs, the wiser your choices will be.

➤ Create your own special itinerary. You don't necessarily need a tour, program, or school to explore your interests while traveling. Do a little research about the place you're going. Find out about the museums, wildlife, handicrafts or whatever it is that makes your heart soar, and build a trip around your passion.

XX
PACKING

On a long journey even a straw weighs heavy.
—*Spanish proverb*

———

BEFORE EVERY TRIP I agonize about what to pack. Should I use my roll-aboard, a sturdy duffel bag, or a big suitcase? Which shoes, coats, clothing should I take? To reduce this stress I begin to tuck items into my bag days before departure. For a short trip, I might pack one or two days in advance. For an adventure trip, such as trekking in the Himalayas, I begin checking my gear (hiking boots, fanny pack, warm coats, flashlights, etc.) weeks before.

Recently I packed in two days for a two-week trip—camping in the Sahara Desert, exploring Morocco's Atlas Mountains, Roman ruins, and imperial cities. How? The adventure travel company who operated the trip sent me a comprehensive packing list. All my gear fit into one duffel bag, and, surprisingly, I didn't have to buy any new clothes or equipment.

I like lists. They keep me organized. I keep several versions in my luggage and highlight in bright yellow the items I continually forget, such as dental floss, belts, and fresh batteries for flashlights. My goal is to pack so efficiently that when I unpack after a trip I discover I have worn or used every item in my bag.

TIPS

➢ When in doubt, leave it out—a good packing motto to help remind you to pack lightly.

➢ Pack doubles of anything you *really* can't live without, like your contact lenses, prescription sunglasses, a copy of your passport, driver's license, or credit card. I even pack two tubes of lip balm and stuff my empty shoes with feminine hygiene supplies.

➤ Pack space-consciously. Roll everything (business suits, blazers, etc.); use dry cleaners' plastic bags between clothing; bring wrinkle-free skirts or pants.

➤ Keep all your luggage organized. Bring zip-lock bags with you. One week into your trip, you'll wish you had brought more. They keep freshly washed but not-quite-dry underwear separated from dry clothes, pills and vitamins separate from snacks. These see-through bags, available in all sizes make it easy to find everything from tampons to batteries to flashlights.

➤ Pack comfy walking shoes! Your shoes must be well worn in before you leave on the trip. Pack extra socks that dry quickly and wick the moisture away from your feet. Bring moleskin in case you develop blisters. Also consider bringing talcum powder to sprinkle in your shoes if you will be walking a lot. This prevents rashes and sweaty feet in hot climates. Wear your bulkiest, heaviest pair of shoes or hiking boots on the plane.

____ ☀ ____

High-quality binoculars are a "must" on wildlife/nature trips, such as those to Alaska and Africa. Each person should have his/her own pair. Affix a label on the binoculars, as well as on the case, so if they're misplaced, they can easily be returned to you.

◆

Marybeth Bond

____ ☀ ____

Clothes wrinkle less in a garment bag if you hang them in the plastic covering from the dry cleaners. Plastic bags from the vegetable department of the supermarket are perfect for shoes.

◆

Laurie Armstrong,
San Francisco, California

➤ Bring one quick-drying travel outfit. Cotton, wool, and linen clothing is impractical, heavy, and outdated for your travel wardrobe. Get with it! New travelwear for women combines practical design with performance fabric. Quick-drying fabrics enable on-the-road wash and wear, while others even remove moisture from your body. This type of fabric is designed for wear on sea-kayaking trips, alpine treks, rafting adventures, and any other activity where you may get wet but must stay dry and warm. Always dress in layers. Shop from a specialized travel catalog or store and splurge on a pair of travel pants (some available with zip-off shorts) and a long-sleeve travel shirt.

➤ Invest in an all-weather travel coat. Although your choice will depend upon the climate of your destination and your adventure activities, a rainproof all-weather coat is essential. It should be light, have many pockets, and feature a hood.

➤ Wear layers of clothing if you are going to a place where the climate changes dramatically from day to night or if you plan lots of outdoor activities.

➤ Always pack your bathing suit. You never know when you'll have an opportunity to swim or hop in a hot tub, and there is no better tension reliever.

➤ Instead of packing a nightgown or pajamas I bring a large t-shirt. It doubles as a cover-up for the beach or pool and I can give it away at the end of the trip.

➤ Adventure gear is different than conventional luggage.

> I never travel without a sarong. Sometimes it can be a skirt, a dress, a beach cover-up, a belt, a carry-all, a bathrobe, or a tablecloth. It is so versatile.
>
> ◆
>
> *Christine Wilson, Portland, Oregon*

The type of principal luggage you will need depends on the type of travel you do. It may accompany you through the streets of Paris or Florence or be tied to the back of a yak or pack animal in the Andes or Himalayas. All destinations, after all, are not alike and your packing needs from trip to trip will most likely vary. Decide what kind of traveler you are: sports and recreation, wilderness, urban, independent or traditional, then research your options. Your travel pack will also have to fit under your seat or in the overhead bin on a plane, in the baggage compartment of a bus, or on the overhead shelf on a train.

➤ What to pack? If you are going on an organized tour, the tour company should provide you with a complete packing list tailored to your destination, its climate, and your activities. If you are traveling on your own, the packing list in the Resources section can become your own master list. Xerox the list and use it for future trips.

One of the smartest things I ever did was have my colors done—not because I'm fashion-conscious, but because dressing in my "palette" allows me to pack light and still look coordinated. From one carry-on bag I can dress for just about any occasion.

♦

Glenda Winders,
San Diego, California

➤ Throw out the hard suitcase. It belongs to the era of the carry-on cosmetic kit. Try a roll-aboard that will fit under the seat or in the overhead. If a roll-aboard isn't for you, try a sturdy duffel bag with built-in compartments. Shop for these in a store specializing in travel luggage.

➤ When buying a travel pack, consider the bag's durability—how much abuse can it take? Look for beefy zippers and finished seams. For the sake of your shoulders, arms, and hands, look for comfy handles and straps.

PACKING FOR THE PLANE

➤ Carry all your medications with you on the plane, in case your checked luggage gets lost or delayed.

➤ My list of items to take on the plane includes reading materials, earplugs, eye shields, neck pillow, socks, a sweater, several nutritious snacks (green apple, granola bar, dried fruit), Chap-stick, toothbrush and toothpaste, extra glasses, pens, stationery, and an address book.

➤ Conquer cold feet. The temperature on airplanes can vary from tropical heat to arctic chill during a flight and you can't count on finding an airline blanket when you need it. Dress in layers, bring a sweater, and pack slipper-socks in your carry-on bag.

Throw a pair of oversize hiking socks into your carry-on bag. Then when you shuck your shoes on long flights, you can keep your feet warm.

◆

Judy Wade, Phoenix, Arizona

Take them out before you stash it overhead or under the seat.

➤ The air circulated in airplane cabins is extremely dry. When traveling by plane, carry lip balm and moisturizer to prevent chapped lips and skin.

➤ Earplugs to the rescue. Inexpensive silicon earplugs reduce the noise on airplanes to help you concentrate on work or reading a good novel. They also regulate the flow of air into your ears and allow you to adapt better to pressure changes. Available at drugstores or airport shops, silicon earplugs (not foam) work the best.

➤ When I pack, I include in my carry-on bag all of my old, unread magazines and my favorite sections of the most recent Sunday *New York Times*. As I read them, I discard them or give them to expatriates or other Americans, who always seem to appreciate my cast-off reading material.

➤ No nylons aboard. Recent tests have shown that when women slide down an airplane's emergency escape ramp, the friction and heat generated from the slide melted their nylon stockings to their legs. Chances are you'll never have to exit a plane this way, but just in case, don't wear pantyhose when you fly.

➤ Identify your bags. More and more people are traveling with black roll-aboard suitcases. Twice someone has mistakenly grabbed my roll-aboard off the baggage-claim carousel. To avoid problems, identify your luggage with something colorful, such as yellow or red ID tags, tie a ribbon around the handle, or wrap a colorful strap around the suitcase.

➤ Provide minimal information on baggage identification tags. I list only my first initial, last name, and geographic area: M. Bond, San Francisco, California. If my bags are lost, airline personnel can locate me through the computer. The information I have provided is too vague for anyone to find my residence, phone number, profession, or place of employment.

➤ Identification tags are often torn off during baggage handling. Be sure to have full identification inside your luggage.

PACKING ESSENTIALS

➤ Put your money in a money belt. You've worked for it. You've saved it. Now protect it and enjoy spending it! Buy a money belt or pouch and wear your valuables close to your heart (or torso). Keep credit cards, travelers' checks, passport, and large bills in it. How much money to bring? Take 20 percent more than you think you'll need. Don't forget to take about twenty one-dollar bills for tips.

➤ Pack a first-aid kit. Don't forget pills, bandages, Imodium, an ample supply of Pepto Bismol and Alka Seltzer tablets, tampons, antibacterial gel, sunscreen, lip balm, and mosquito repellent. Another must is an all-purpose antibiotic, such as Ciproflaxacin, which can be used for serious traveler's diarrhea, upper respiratory problems, and more. A prescription is necessary, so consult with your doctor.

➤ Emergen-C or Airborne—many experienced travelers won't leave home without one of these dietary supplements. Those powdered vitamin packets, available at health food stores, are essential in any tropical climate because they replace electrolytes and fluids lost through perspiration. If you have treated your water with iodine, it will improve the taste.

➤ Bring a small bottle of anti-bacterial gel. Then you can always wash your hands before meals and after pit stops.

➤ Pack a small flashlight and leave it on your bedside table. If you awake during the night you won't have to fumble for the light switch. If you have a roommate you won't wake her/him if you use your flashlight to go to the bathroom and you can read in bed if your roommate wants to go to sleep before you.

➤ Duct tape to the rescue. Have you ever had a sandal strap break or the handle fall off your suitcase mid-trip? Pack a long strip of duct tape for unexpected repairs. Just wrap it around a pen and tuck it in your bag.

➤ Shampoo—from hair to hosiery. If you're staying in relatively nice hotels, don't bother to pack washing detergent. The shampoo provided by your hotel can be used to wash out underwear or hosiery.

➤ If you're traveling on a budget and your hotels are unlikely to provide shampoo, pack a Zip-lock bag full of detergent for washing your clothes.

➤ Pack extra batteries for your cameras. If, by accident, you leave the shutter open or flash on overnight, your battery will be dead in the morning. You may not find the size and brand of battery you need easily.

➤ Pack a drain stopper. Travel nuts know how important a drain stopper can be! How else can you take a bath or plug up the sink to wash clothes, if the place you're staying doesn't have one? The flat type are best to cover a variety of sink drains and are available at hardware stores.

➤ Pack an extra nylon duffel inside your luggage to store items in a hotel in the event you travel to other cities and want to leave a bag behind. It is also useful as an extra piece of luggage to carry home purchases.

➤ Take along photos of your home, pets, and family as well as colorful postcards of your hometown. Postcards are easy gifts, and personal photos help you share your world. A frisbee, puppet, or colored pens and pencils will win you friends.

➤ Pack positive, inspiring books that you can trade with other travelers. Look for women's travel narratives.

➤ Pack a sense of humor, no matter what else you bring.

The first things into my suitcase are always the bandannas—at least a half-dozen per trip, in a variety of bright colors. Nothing so light, so easy to pack, has ever played so many roles, saved so many days. The simple cotton squares serve as headbands when hiking; cooling, damp neckerchiefs when worn wet in a steamy jungle; fast-drying washcloths in all those hotels and hostels that don't provide them; or washcloths in camp that can be quick-dipped in a stream and quick-dried, draped over a branch or bush. They are often the only end-of-the-day solution to "hat head" or wilted beach hair, a plague I am prone to even in the desert. Thus, my bandannas go wherever my passport goes. And, invariably, I give the lavenders and yellows and tie-dyes away along the way, coming home even lighter than I left.

♦

Paula McDonald, Baja California, Mexico

XXI
THE FINAL WORD

Through travel I first became aware of the outside world; it was through travel that I found my own introspective way into becoming a part of it.

—*Eudora Welty*

"HOW HAS TRAVEL CHANGED YOUR LIFE?" someone once asked me in an interview. Travel has changed me in many ways. It's made me more aware of the world around me. It's brought extraordinary people into my life. It's taught me to give up control. It's deepened my sense of awe. In answering the question, though, I realized the single most important way travel has affected me: It's made me deeply comfortable with *myself*. Before I traveled around the world at age twenty-nine, I had never gone to a movie or out to eat alone. Now, after years of travel and risk taking, I savor the moments I have to myself. I have learned to listen deeply to myself, and to have confidence in my choices. I am a Gutsy Woman.

Gutsy does not mean fearless. On the contrary—it means coming close enough to our fears that we realize the depth of our courage.

And through travel, we come to know and summon that courage. For as we leave our well-trod terrain and all that is familiar behind, we leave our comfort zones. Whether communicating in a new language, finding our way through a foreign city, or tasting strange new food, travel challenges and stretches us. As we test ourselves, we break through limiting ideas of ourselves. We discover that we are more than what we thought; we can do more than we imagined. We can break with tradition, try on new roles, cross boundaries imposed by society or the routines of our day-to-day lives. As we travel, we reclaim our sense of self and strength. Travel takes us to the core of ourselves, and it changes us.

My hope, thus, is that the tips, wisdom, and personal anecdotes presented in this third edition of *Gutsy Women* will help inform and illuminate your own unique path—the one that draws you boldly out into the world and, inevitably, bravely into yourself. I hope that the voices of the many women quoted in this book have inspired you to crack open your own fears and discover the treasures within.

So be a Gutsy Woman—you know you already are! Take a trip—it doesn't matter if it's a monthlong trek in the Himalayas or a day-long excursion to a local beach. What's important is trying something new, something compelling and maybe even a little scary. Something you've dreamed about. Whatever it is, try it. See how it feels. See what you learn about yourself. It may be something you never imagined. Something wonderful. Something surprising. Something...*gutsy*.

XXII
RESOURCES AND REFERENCES

SERVICES AND ORGANIZATIONS

Women's Tour Services

AAA Sojourns
www.csaa.com

A Broad Adventure
www.abroadadventure.com

Adventure Associates
www.adventureassociates.net

Adventure Cycling Tours &
Vacations for Women
www.femtoursguide.com

Adventure Divas
www.adventuredivas.com/tours

Adventures in Good Company
www.adventuresingoodcompany.
com

Adventures in New Zealand for
Women
www.driftwooddreamers.com

Adventures in Perspective
www.livingadventure.com

AdventurePlanet
www.adventureplanet.com

AdventureWomen
www.adventurewomen.com

Adventurous Wench
www.adventurouswench.com

American Woman Road & Travel
www.roadandtravel.com

Annapurna Journeys
www.goldenhilltravel.co.uk/nepal/
annapurna-journeys.html

Arctic Ladies
www.arcticladies.com

Armstrong & Hedges
http://teagardentravel.com

Artista
www.artistacreative.com

The Association of Women Travel
Executives, London
www.awte-london.co.uk

Astra
www.astragreece.com

Azores Walks
www.azoreswalks.com

Babes in the Backcountry
www.babesinthebackcountry.com

Bev Gruber's Everyday Gourmet
Traveler
www.gourmetravel.com

Blue Moon Explorations
http://home.cio.net/bluemoon

Broad Horizons
www.broadhorizonsnetwork.com

Bushwise Women
www.bushwise.co.nz

Call of the Wild
www.callwild.com

Canadian Woman Traveller
www.cwtraveller.ca

Canyon Calling Tours
www.canyoncalling.com

Caribbean Bike & Adventure
Tours
www.caribbeanbiketours.com

Chicks with Picks, Chicks with
Sticks
www.chickswithpicks.net

Chimo Club Toronto
www.chimoclubtoronto.org

Cloud Canyon Expeditions
www.cloudcanyon.com

Costa Rican Luxury Vacation
www.vacationscostarica.com

Country Walkers
www.countrywalkers.com

Destinations Europe
www.womens-tours.com

Direct Approach Golf School
www.golfschoolpi.com

Diva Expeditions
www.divaexpeditions.com

EarthWise Journeys
http://home.teleport.com/
~earthwyz

Ela Brasil Tours
www.elabrasil.com

Eliotropica Travelling
www.eliotropica.com

Elderhostel
www.elderhostel.org

Equinox Wilderness Expeditions
www.equinoxexpeditions.com

Eurynome Journeys of Leisure
Markets: Travel Adventures for
Women
www.wanderwoman.com

Explorations in Travel
www.exploretravel.com

Fresh Tracks
www.freshtracks.ca

GATE
www.gate-travel.org

Genuine Romance Adventures
www.GenuineRomanceAdven-
tures.com

Global Fitness Adventures
www.globalfitnessadventures.
com

Going Places!
www.goingplacestours.com

Go-Outdoors
www.go-outdoors.ca

GORP Travel
www.gorptravel.com

Grape Adventures
www.grapeadventures.com

Gutsy Gals Travel
www.gutsygalstravel.com

Gutsy Women Travel
www.gutsywomentravel.com

High Wild & Lonesome
www.hwl.net

The Historic Pines Ranch
www.historicpines.com

Holiday Expeditions
www.bikeraft.com

Il Chiostro
www.ilchiostro.com

Journey Weavers Educational
Travel
www.journeyweavers.com

Journeys International
www.journeys-intl.com

Journeys of the Spirit
www.journeysofthespirit.com

Inspiring Ireland
www.inspiringireland.com/
CromCastleRetreat.htm

Las Olas
www.surflasolas.com

Las Verdes
www.golflasverdes.com

Loners on Wheels
www.lonersonwheels.com

Mama Tembo Tours
www.mamatembotours.com

Mariah Wilderness Expeditions
www.mariahwomen.com

Menopausal Tours
www.menopausaltours.com

Mind Over Mountains
www.mindovermountains.com

Mountain Spirit Adventures
www.mountainspiritadventures.
com

Newage Travel
www.newage-travel.com

Olivia Cruises & Resorts
www.olivia.com

Ontdek Kenya
www.ontdekkenya.com

Outdoor Beyond
www.outdoorbeyond.com

Painting Tours in Italy
www.portray.it

PanTours of Australasia
www.pantoursindia.com

Paris du Jour
www.parisdujour.com

Peaceful Choices
http://internet.cybermesa.com/
~innerpeace

Phyllis Trips
www.phyllistrips.com

RVing Women
www.rvingwomen.org

Sacred Earth Journeys
www.sacredearthjourneys.ca

Sacred Journeys for Women
www.sacredjourneys.com

Sacred Sites Tours
www.sacredsitestours.com

Sanddrifters
www.sanddrifters.com

Seagypsy
www.seagypsysailing.com

Senior Women's Travel
www.poshnosh.com

Sherri Griffith Expeditions
www.griffithexp.com

Shesailing
www.shesailing.nl

Shop Around Tours
www.shoparoundtours.com

Sights and Soul Travels
www.sightsandsoul.com

Sierra Club
www.sierraclub/org/outings/
national

Sila Sojourns
www.silasojourns.com

Soul Purpose Adventures
www.soulpurpose.bc.ca

Soul Trekking
www.soultrekking.com

Sounds & Furies Productions
www.soundsandfuries.com

South Sea Mermaid Tours
www.southseamermaids.co.nz

Surf Goddess Retreats
www.surfgoddessretreats.com

Tanguera Tours
www.tangueratours.com

Tea Garden Traveler
www.teagardentravel.com

Tiger Travel
www.tigertravel.co.uk

Tours Explore
www.toursexplore.com

Towanda Women
www.towanda.org

Transcend Travel Switzerland
www.transcendtravel.com

Transition Counseling Services
www.transitioncounselingser-
vices.com

Travel with Women
www.travelwithwomen.com

Trips for Women
www.tripsforwomen.com

A Twisty Road
www.twistyroad.com

Unleashed Adventures
www.unleashedadventures.com

Valentine Travel
www.valentinetravel.com

Walking Women Holidays
www.walkingwomen.com

Well Arranged Travel
www.wellarrangedtravel.com

West Coast Women Adventures
www.westcoastwomen.ca

Wild Women Expeditions
www.wildwomenexp.com

Woman Tours
www.womantours.com

Womanship
www.womanship.com

WomanWalkers Travel Service
www.womenwalkers.com

Woman's World Travel
www.womansworldtravel.com

Woman Xplore
www.womenxplore.com

Women in Florence
www.womeninflorence.com

Women's Only Mountain Biking
www.womensonly.com

Women Summit
www.womensummit.com

Women's Quest
www.womensquest.com

Women Traveling Together
www.women-traveling.com

Women Travel New Zealand
www.womentravel.co.nz

Women's Travel Club
www.womenstravelclub.com

Women's Travel Network
www.womentravelnetwork.ca

Women Travelling
www.womentravelling.com

Women Welcome Women
www.womenwelcomewomen.
org.uk

The World Outdoors
www.theworldoutdoors.com

Mature/Senior Travel

Elderhostel
www.elderhostel.org

ElderTreks
www.eldertreks.com

Explorations in Travel
www.exploretravel.com

Folkways Travel
1-800-225-4666

Grand Circle Tracel
www.gct.com

Interhostel
www.learn.unh.edu/interhostel

Overseas Adventure Travel
www.oattravel.com

Saga International Holidays
www.sagaholidays.com

Senior Women's Travel
www.poshnosh.com

Walking the World
www.walkingtheworld.com

Volunteer/Travel Opportunities

American Hiking Society
Volunteer Vacation
www.americanhiking.org

Cross-Cultural Solutions
www.crossculturalsolutions.org

Earthwatch
www.earthwatch.org

Global Exchange
www.globalexchange.org

Global Service Corps
www.globalservicecorps.org

Global Volunteers
www.globalvolunteers.org

Globe Aware
www.globeaware.org

Habitat for Humanity
www.habitat.org

Sierra Club
www.sierraclub.org/outings/
national/service

Tropical Adventures Volunteer
Tours
www.mytropicaladventure.com

Volunteer International
www.volunteerinternational.org

World Teach
www.worldteach.org

Homestays

American International
Homestays
www.aihtravel.com/homestays

Servas International
www.usservas.org

Fear of Flying

Fearless Flyer Classes
www.fearless-flight.com/fear-of-
flying/seminars.php

Pegasus Fear of Flying
Foundation
www.pegasus-fear-fly.com

MISCELLANEOUS
RESOURCES

Credit Card Advice

American Express
800-528-4800 in the U.S.
623-492-8596 collect from
abroad

Diner's Club
800-346-3779 in the U.S.
702-797-5532 collect from
abroad

Discover
800-347-2683
(Discover is not accepted outside
the U.S.)

MasterCard
800-622-7747 in the U.S.
314-542-7111 collect from
abroad

Visa
800-336-8472 in the U.S.
410-581-9994 collect from
abroad

Traveler's Check Advice

American Express
800-221-7282

Citicorp
800-645-6556 in the U.S.
813-623-1709 collect from
abroad

Visa
800-227-6811 or 800-732-1322
in the U.S.
44-17-33-318-949 collect from
abroad

PACKING LIST

CLOTHING	HYGIENE	MEDICAL
___ belts	___ body cream	___ antihistamines
___ blouses	___ brush/comb	___ antibiotic
___ bras	___ dental floss	ointment
___ boots	___ deodorant	___ antiseptic skin
___ coats	___ face soap	cleanser
___ dresses	___ foot powder	___ Band-aids
___ gloves	___ Kleenex	___ birth control
___ hats	___ lip balm	___ contact lenses
___ jackets	___ magnifying	and supplies
___ jeans	mirror	___ cotton swabs
___ long t-shirt	___ makeup	___ diarrhea
___ panties	___ moleskin	medicine
___ pantyhose	___ nail brush	___ insect repellent
___ rain/sun hat	___ nail clippers	___ motion sickness
___ raincoat	___ nail file	remedy
___ scarves	___ nail polish	___ muscle relaxant
___ shirts	remover	___ nasal spray
___ shoes, dress	___ razor/blades	___ Pepto Bismol/
___ shoes, walking	___ shampoo/con-	Alka Seltzer
___ shorts	ditioner	___ prescription
___ skirts	___ sunblock	glasses (extra
___ slacks	___ surgical face	pair and copy
___ slippers	mask	of prescription
___ socks	___ or kerchief	___ prescription
___ suits	___ tampons	medications
___ sweat suit	___ toothbrush	___ sleeping pills
___ sweaters	___ toothpaste	___ Sting Stop™ gel
___ swimsuits	___ tweezers	___ thermometer

DOCUMENTS

___ address book
___ credit cards
___ driver's license
___ family pictures
    (in plastic
    cover)
___ maps
___ passport/visas
___ passport photos
    (include extras)
___ photocopies of
    passport/visas
___ student ID card
___ travel insurance
___ travel tickets
___ travelers'
    checks

MISCELLANEOUS

___ alarm clock
___ batteries
___ calculator
___ camera/film
___ cash
___ clothesline
___ corkscrew
___ earplugs
___ electrical
    converter &
    adapter plugs
___ eyeshades
___ filmshield
___ flashlight
___ games/
    playing cards
___ guidebooks
___ highlighter pen
    (to mark maps)
___ journal
___ laundry deter-
    gent/Woolite
___ luggage locks
    (combination)
___ luggage tags
___ pens/pencils
___ phrase book
___ pillowcase
    (doubles as
    laundry bag)
___ pocket
    calculator
___ reading material

___ rubber bands
___ rubber door
    stopper
___ safety pins
___ scissors
___ sewing kit
___ stationery
___ sunglasses
___ tape recorder
    & tapes
___ watch
___ water bottle
___ whistle
___ zip-lock bags

INDEX OF CONTRIBUTORS

Acknowledgments

I have been tolerated and my absences in mind and body forgiven by my patient, loving husband Gary and my heart's great joy, my daughters Julieclaire and Annalyse.

Three decades of my own travel experiences and a broad wealth of other travelers' wisdom have gone into the making of *Gutsy Women*. I couldn't have completed this book without help.

My heartfelt thanks to two talented writers and editors: Lisa Bach and Natanya Pearlman. They created structure from chaos and added wit, wisdom, thoughtful editing, and eloquent text to this book. They shared their writing expertise, insights, and humor with me. We share a mission and believe passionately in empowering and inspiring women to travel.

My heartfelt thanks to those who also helped with *Gutsy Women*: James O'Reilly, Larry Habegger, Susan Brady, and Christy Quinto at Travelers' Tales.

Simply, sincerely, thank you to all of my travel buddies, writer colleagues, supportive friends, mentors, and role models who have inspired, advised, and encouraged me.

About the Author

Marybeth Bond has not always been a Gutsy Woman. At summer camp, when she was ten years old, she was nicknamed "Misty" because she had a bad case of homesickness. Not one of her counselors would have predicted a traveling future for her. However, several decades later, Marybeth has hiked, cycled, climbed, dived, and kayaked her way through more than seventy countries around the world, from the depths of the Flores Sea to the summit of Mount Kilimanjaro. She studied in Paris for four years, earned two degrees, and had a business career in marketing.

At twenty-nine, she took off again, this time to travel alone around the world. These two years of travel changed her life. She met her future husband, an American, in Kathmandu, Nepal, and she returned to begin a new career as a writer, consultant, and lecturer. Since then she has given lectures around the world at such venues as the Explorers Club and Asia Society in New York.

Marybeth's first book, *A Woman's World,* is a best-seller and won the Lowell Thomas Gold Medal for Best Travel Book from the Society of American Travel Writers Foundation. It is an eloquent collection of women's writing that paints a rich portrait of what it means to be a woman today.

Marybeth was a featured guest on the Oprah Winfrey Show, with her book *Gutsy Women*. As a nationally recognized travel expert and media personality, Marybeth has appeared on CBS News, CNN, ABC, NBC, FOX TV, and National Public Radio. She was the "Smart Traveler" radio host for the nationally syndicated Outside Radio show and the travel expert/columnist for the Travel Channel on ivillage.com, the women's online network. She was also the "travel expert" for CBS's Evening Magazine. She is currently the Adventure Editor for *travelgirl magazine* and the Spokesperson for AAA, Northern California. Follow along with her at www.gutsytraveler.com.

Marybeth has two children, a husband, and a dog and lives in Northern California. She travels as much as she can—with her children, her husband, girlfriends, mother, or alone.

Other Books by Marybeth Bond

A Woman's World

A Woman's Passion for Travel

Gutsy Mamas

A Mother's World

A Woman's Europe

A Woman's Asia

50 Best Girlfriends Getaways

A Woman's World Again